Colin Shindler is an academic and writer. He is Reader in Israeli and Modern Jewish Studies at the School of Oriental and African Studies, University of London, where he teaches courses on both Zionism and the ██████ ████████ ████ books include *Ploughshares into S.. ██████ ██████ low of the Intifada* (1991); *The ██████ ██████ ud and the Zionist Dream* (20.. ██████ ry *Zionism: Nationalism and th.. ██ Right* (2006). He is a regular contributor to the national and international media on the tortuous struggle between Israelis and Palestinians. He grew up in Hackney, in London, and studied chemistry at university. He is married with four grown-up children and three grandchildren.

Cover image:
The star (shield) of David between two blue lines on a white background was formally adopted as the flag of the Zionist movement in 1933. Although it was first displayed by the early Jewish settlers in Palestine as far back as 1885. The two blue lines were taken from the design of the *talit*, the Jewish prayer shawl. In more recent times, the lines have erroneously been attributed in Arab commentary to representing the Biblical borders of the Land of Israel – from the Nile to the Euphrates.

SERIES EDITOR: TONY MORRIS

Available now

What Do Astrologers Believe? by Nicholas Campion
What Do Buddhists Believe? by Tony Morris
What Do Christians Believe? by Malcolm Guite
What Do Druids Believe? by Philip Carr-Gomm
What Do Existentialists Believe? by Richard Appignanesi
What Do Greens Believe? by Joe Smith
What Do Jews Believe? by Edward Kessler
What Do Muslims Believe? by Ziauddin Sardar
What Do Pagans Believe? by Graham Harvey

Forthcoming

What Do Catholics Believe? by Leonie Caldecott
What Do Hindus Believe? by Rachel Dwyer

What Do ZIONISTS Believe?

Colin Shindler

Granta Books

London

Granta Publications, 2/3 Hanover Yard, Noel Road, London N1 8BE

First published in Great Britain by Granta Books 2007

A CIP catalogue record for this book
is available from the British Library.

1 3 5 7 9 10 8 6 4 2

ISBN 978-1-86207-836-9

Typeset by M Rules

Printed and bound in Great Britain by
Bookmarque Limited, Croydon, Surrey

*This book is dedicated to
the memory of Cecil Zarach (1915–2001)
who understood*

Be on your guard against the ruling power; for they who exercise it draw no man near to them except for their own interests; appearing as friends when it is to their own advantage, they stand not by a man in the hour of his need. (Rabban Gamliel, *Ethics of the Fathers*)

Contents

Acknowledgements

I would like to express my gratitude to David Hirsh, Shalom Lappin and Yossi Mekelberg for reading through the drafts of this work and for providing valuable insights. I would also like to acknowledge the contributions of the many students at SOAS, University of London, who have taken my course on the history of Zionism. They will no doubt see in this book some of the ideas and responses that came up during class discussion. I would also like to express my appreciation for all his support to Tony Morris, the editor of this series. Lastly I would like to thank my wonderful wife, Jean, for her understanding and support in all my endeavours.

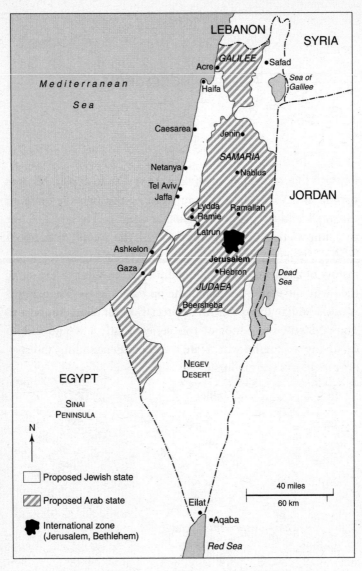

The proposed partition of Palestine by the UN in 1947

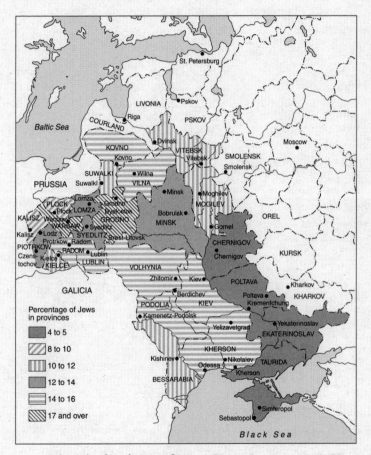

The Pale of Settlement of Jews in Tsarist Russia in 1913

1

Who is a Zionist?

Between Fantasy and Demonization?

Zionism is seen in pejorative terms today, as a manifestation of political reaction and religious obscurantism in Israel. At worst 'Zionist' is used as a term of abuse, an epithet to be hurled at anyone who does not see the Israel–Palestine conflict in monochrome.

The Liverpudlian comedian Alexei Sayle asks: 'If the Zionists wanted a homeland, why didn't they take a piece of Germany? The answer is, of course, that Arabs, then and now, were not considered fully human by the Zionists . . . and therefore could be murdered without qualms.'[1] Perhaps the political views of stand-up comics shouldn't merit the same importance as their jokes. But in all likelihood Sayle's comment represents a profound and probably widespread ignorance about Zionism and the tortuous Israel–Palestine conflict.

The grassroots mass movement Peace Now, which has a long history of protest against Israeli government support for the Jewish settlements established in the territories conquered in the 1967 war, is never characterized as 'Zionist' even though it proclaims such an affiliation. Yossi Beilin, the architect of the Oslo Accords (1993) and the Geneva Agreement (2003), a joint Israeli–Palestinian initiative in search of a genuine two-state solution, has unequivocally stated that he is a Zionist. Members of 'Courage to Refuse', the conscripts who refused to serve in the West Bank and Gaza during the current Intifada, the Palestinian uprising, similarly do not disavow Zionism. Even though Zionism is a defining feature of a large section of the Israeli peace camp, it is often portrayed in the Western media as synonymous with occupation, violation of human rights and military aggression. These contemporary examples of selective denial are characteristic of the poor level of understanding about Zionism.

Zionism today is also defined by – and blamed for – the exodus of Arabs from Palestine during the war of 1948. For the Zionist Jews, it was a war of independence. For the Palestinian Arabs, it was 'al Nakhba', 'the catastrophe'. The war at first was a civil war with the Palestinians and then a conflict with the invading armies of the surrounding Arab states, which wished to eliminate Israel at birth. Although United Nations Resolution 181 of November 1947 had suggested a partition into two states, only the Zionists accepted the proposal. Arab nationalists never accepted that the Jews had a right to national self-determination and viewed Zionism as merely an offshoot of Western imperialism. Islamists in the Muslim Brotherhood saw Zionism as simply a poisonous implant on Muslim soil. The Zionists therefore viewed the war as one of survival, of 'them or us'. Between 600,000 and 700,000 Palestinian Arabs fled – some of them were expelled – and over 100,000 remained in the new state of Israel. In mid-June 1948 the new Israeli government refused to readmit Palestinian refugees because they feared that they would act as a fifth column and nullify a bitterly fought military victory.

But was the tragedy of the Palestinians an inevitable outcome of Zionist ideology? Could it have ended differently in different circumstances? The traditional Zionist narrative argues that it could indeed have been very different if wiser Arab counsel had prevailed. Conversely, Palestinian nationalists today proclaim that Zionist ideology is the root cause of all Palestine's disasters and that the expulsion of 1948 was a preordained outcome.

Benny Morris, the first historian to gain access to newly available Israeli archives in the 1980s, upset both Israeli and Palestinian purveyors of the black-and-white version of history. He punctured the Israeli myth that the Palestinians left of their own accord and that no one was expelled. But he also demolished the Palestinian myth that everyone was expelled. Morris wrote: 'The Palestinian refugee problem was born of war, not by design, Jewish or Arab. It was largely a by-product of Arab and Jewish fears and of the protracted, bitter fighting that characterised the first Israel–Arab war; in smaller part, it was the deliberate creation of Jewish and Arab military commanders and politicians.'[2] He argued that the option of transferring the Arabs in pre-war Palestine occupied the minds of at least a few Zionist officials who confined their thoughts to their diaries and private letters, but for the overwhelming majority, as liberals and socialists, it remained morally dubious.[3]

While thinking about transfer certainly increased in the 1930s in the general Zionist mindset, this was 'not tantamount to pre-planning' and there was no policy or a master plan for expulsion.[4] Even Vladimir Jabotinsky, the leader of the Zionist Right, formally condemned transfer.[5] It was the British, in the Peel Commission Report of 1937, who took the lead in advocating the movement of Arabs out of the proposed Jewish state and Jews out of the proposed Arab state. In the inter-war years the exchange of populations was seen as a rational method of resolving inter-communal conflicts such as the long-running Greek–Turkish imbroglio.

Zionism sought to create a place where Jews could attain political independence and instigate a national renaissance of the Jewish people. The early Zionist pioneers in Palestine had believed, perhaps naively, that Jews and Arabs could somehow cooperate for the benefit of all. The violence of the Arab Revolt in the 1930s and the unwillingness of the Palestinian Arab leadership to contemplate any meaningful compromise made many Jews believe that the conflict was a zero-sum game. While the Jews were divided on the question of the partition of Palestine, the Arabs were united in their rejection of it. With the onset of war in December 1947 the worst-case scenario had come to pass and while there was no master plan for expulsion, the issue of transfer was already in the Zionist psyche. The unpredictability of war took over with terrible results.

Out of the conflicting narratives of Jew and Arab, the megaphone war between Israelis and Palestinians has reduced a complex history to a hollow sound bite. One of its casualties has been any serious consideration of Zionism. Instead Zionists have been often deemed responsible in some left-wing publications in Europe and in the mainstream Arab media for orchestrating many acts of terrorism in the world – from the killing of Westerners in Saudi Arabia to the massacre of children in Beslan. In 2001 conspiracy theorists throughout the world were adamant in their belief that 'Zionists' were behind the tragedy of the Twin Towers on 11 September 2001. In certain parts of the Arab world in particular, 'the crimes of Zionism' have reached hitherto unimaginable levels of fantasy.

This is not a new phenomenon. During the 1960s the Soviet Union imitated McCarthyite America in locating 'Zionists under the bed' for each and every misdemeanour. Accusations of Communist subversion in the USA were paralleled by belief in Zionist sedition in the USSR. 'Zionists' were behind the Prague Spring of Dubček's 'Communism with a human face'. 'Zionists' helped Nazis murder Jews when Germany invaded the USSR in 1941. Jack Ruby, the killer of Lee Harvey Oswald, Kennedy's assassin, was a 'Zionist'. And, of course, so was Mao Zedong.

Occasionally such Stalinist stupidity surfaces as throwaway comments in far-Left publications in Europe. The dark force of 'international Zionism' was held responsible in many a broadsheet for manipulating the Bush administration into its controversial invasion of Iraq. Jewish neo-conservatives in the administration, it was implied, operated with the encouragement and full approval of the Sharon government to push the United States into the Iraqi quagmire. All misleading information on WMDs in Iraq had, it was surmised, originated in Israel.[6]

Regimes opposed to the Bush administration find 'Zionists' a convenient target. Iran's Supreme Leader, Ayatollah Ali Khamenei, therefore voiced the opinion that the 'Zionists' were behind the publication of the offensive cartoons of the Prophet in Denmark in 2005.[7] When the Jewish filmmaker Jonathan Jakubowicz made a film about social conditions in his native Venezuela, he was – to his surprise – attacked by government officials who commented that the film had been sponsored by the CIA and 'the Zionist conspiracy against [President Hugo] Chavez'.[8] Following a criticism of Iran, the *Teheran Times* even discovered that *Al Jazeera* had been founded by 'Zionists'.[9]

This mindset has particularly influenced the European Left, who, ironically, strongly supported Zionism and the idea of a Jewish state in Palestine after World War II. Today Israeli Jews are depicted as well-to-do white Europeans and the Palestinian Arabs as the exploited and dispossessed of the developing world. Thus the Mayor of London, Ken Livingstone, was happy to embrace and endorse the Muslim scholar Sheikh Yussef al Qaradawi in July 2004, yet the cleric was not averse to blaming 'Zionists' for the bombing of the Shiite shrine of the 'hidden Imam' at Samarra in Iraq some two years later.[10]

There are some on the Left who believe that anti-Zionism can never be equated with anti-Semitism. Some simplistically believe that accusations of anti-Semitism are merely a subterfuge to deflect attacks on the Israeli occupation of the West Bank.[11] This denies a history of anti-Semitic figures on the Left such as Bakunin, Proudhon and Dühring. 'Zionists' is sometimes used as code for Jews, just as 'rootless cosmopolitans' was employed in Stalin's time in the Soviet Union.[12] There are Islamists, however, who are clear and direct in their anti-Semitism. Sheikh Hassan Nasrallah, the secretary-general of Lebanon's Hezbollah, pointed out: 'If we searched the entire world for a person, more cowardly, despicable, weak and feeble in psyche, mind, ideology and religion, we would not find anyone like the Jew. Notice, I do not say the Israeli.'[13]

The very idea that Zionism was never monolithic does not occur to its detractors. There were certainly those Zionists on the far Right, such as Abba Achimeir, who believed that Zionism should imitate Mussolini's Italy. This, of course, took place long before Italy's anti-Semitic laws were enacted, but even so, the nationalist Zionist leader Vladimir Jabotinsky reacted vehemently to being called 'Duce' and to the very idea of abandoning democracy. 'Buffaloes,' he remarked, 'follow a "leader". Civilized men have no "leaders".'[14] Other Zionist radicals thought that Sinn Fein was a good model. Jabotinsky's Revisionist movement warmed to neither, but looked instead to Garibaldi and the

Italian Risorgimento. Socialist Zionism had its Marxist wing as well as a social-democratic one. Indeed Ben-Gurion's party, Achdut Ha'avodah, held a closed session to eulogize Lenin after his death in 1924.[15] Political Zionists saw the creation of the Jewish state as the prime concern. Practical Zionists, on the other hand, viewed the development of a national community as the central task in hand. Hashomer Hatzair, the Marxist Zionist movement embraced bi-nationalism as late as 1947. Others disdained such labels and assiduously worked the land in Tolstoyan fashion. At the foundation of their movement, most religious Zionists did not invoke the coming of the Messiah and would have been puzzled at the redemptionist zeal of the religious settlers on the West Bank a century later. Neither did all religious Zionists believe in the imperative for a greater Israel. Hapoel Hamizrachi, the labouring religious Zionist movement, supported the plan to partition Palestine in 1947.

'Zions' were located in areas as far flung as Argentina, Alaska, Angola, Ecuador, French Guyana, the New Hebrides and Tasmania. A recent book carried the title *States for the Jews: Uganda, Birobidzhan and 34 Other Plans*.[16] Many early Zionists at the end of the nineteenth century, however, advocated a Jewish national home within Palestine – the geographical location of ancient Israel. It was to be a homeland guaranteed by the international community, with land purchased from local notables. Zionist pioneers in Palestine saw themselves as colonizers and not colonialists. They argued that they were there by historic right and not on the sufferance of others. Unlike European imperialists, they did not come with armies, ready to expropriate the land and dispossess its inhabitants, but with hoes and pitchforks to cultivate the soil. They perceived Zionism as the return of the Jews to the Land of Israel and the construction of a just society in their ancient homeland.

Zionism was a movement of national liberation, modelled on nineteenth-century European nationalism and the French revolutionary tradition. It sought to both normalize and modernize the situation of the marginalized Jewish people.[17] For the religious, it was the beginning of redemption and the onset of the messianic age. For Marxist Zionists, it was an opportunity to rectify the abnormal socio-economic structure of the Jews in the Diaspora by settling them on the land. For idealists and dreamers, it was the construction of a perfect society based on socialist theory merged with themes of social justice cemented in the biblical teachings of the prophets. Others ridiculed all this as utopian and proposed a modern technological, capitalist state. The Hebrew Republic which arose as the state of Israel in May 1948 embraced all these possibilities.

Who, today, is a Zionist? This is difficult to define since the understanding of Zionism has changed over the years. Originally a Zionist was someone who emigrated to Israel and participated in the construction of the country and in the forging of a just society. A Zionist could also be someone whose intention was to settle in Israel in the future but for the time being decided to remain in his country of domicile. American Jews – immigrant founders of their country – argued that there was a profound difference between exile and Diaspora. Some came to extol the virtues of the Diaspora: 'The Jews have probably spent far more years of our historical lifetime in the Diaspora than in our own country and it makes no sense to characterize as abnormal a way of life that accounts for more than half of a people's historical existence. Diaspora is simply a characteristic condition of our history; paradoxically it might even be said to be more characteristic than statehood which we share with hundreds of other peoples.'[18]

Some have argued that a major failure of Zionism was the decision of a majority of Diaspora Jews to remain in their country of domicile. Today 38% of all Jews live in Israel. While few Jews left North America or Western Europe, a million former Soviet citizens emigrated to Israel in the 1990s. New arrivals came mainly from countries of persecution and partial integration. As David Ben-Gurion, Israel's founding Prime Minister, commented as far back as the 1960s: 'The title of Zionist now embraces entirely different things among which there is no connection, and to speak of Zionism per se has no real meaning.'[19]

While classical Zionism had ended with the establishment of the state in 1948, it was unclear what had emerged instead. In the 1950s Ben-Gurion extended the term 'Zionism' – formerly the property of the Zionists – to include the entire Jewish people. Such Zionization served not only to cement Jewish solidarity with Israel, but also to provide a political hinterland for the policies of successive Israeli governments. Yet Ben-Gurion was not averse to using both arguments at different times for different purposes. At the 25th Zionist Congress in 1961 he quoted the Talmudic dictum that 'he who resides outside the Land of Israel is as one who has no God'.[20]

For Diaspora Jews, Zionism today means a broad identification with Israel. In a survey of Jewish identity in Britain in 2004, 47% of those questioned agreed with the proposition 'I am a Zionist'. Twenty-six per cent were unsure and 27% disagreed. Yet when it came to identifying with Israel rather than with Zionist ideology, the choice was much more decisive. Seventy-eight per cent agreed with the statement 'I care deeply about Israel'. Seventeen per cent were unsure and only 5% disagreed.[21]

No doubt this strong identification with Israel is, in part, a reaction to the sense of abandonment of the Jews during the Holocaust. For Jews, 'Never Again' is no mere slogan but a defining sensitivity. The Allies may have won the war, but the Jews certainly lost it. In December 1946 Chaim Weizmann, the first President of Israel, addressed the delegates of the 22nd Zionist Congress. Noting the yawning gaps in the audience since the previous pre-war meeting, he commented: 'Now in the light of past and present events the bitter truth must be spoken. We feared too little and we hoped too much. We underestimated the bestiality of the enemy; we overestimated the humanity, the wisdom, the sense of justice of our friends.'[22]

The murder of six million Jews transformed the outlook of Jews worldwide. Zionists, anti-Zionists, atheists, ultra-orthodox, socialists, capitalists, rich, poor – the Nazis made no exceptions. All Jews automatically became survivors. In his poem 'Shema' Primo Levi addressed those who were not there, who did not bear witness, those 'who live secure / in your warm houses / who returning at evening, find / hot food and friendly faces'. Jews in Britain asked what would have happened if Hitler had crossed the channel. Would Britain's Jews have been protected, as happened in Denmark and Bulgaria? Or would British collaborators in abundance have aided the Nazis? For a majority of Jews and many non-Jews, the abandonment and slaughter of Europe's Jews changed attitudes towards Zionism. Levi's poem, written in January 1946, ended:

Consider that this has been
I commend these words to you
Engrave them on your hearts
When you are in your house, when you walk on your way
When you go to bed, when you rise:
Repeat them to your children.

Or may your house crumble,
Disease render you powerless,
Your offspring avert their faces from you.[23]

'Shema' is the Hebrew for 'hear' or 'listen' – and many ordinary people did. For most Jews and for the Left in particular there was almost a moral imperative to open the gates and allow Jews to leave for Palestine. The *Guardian* endorsed the call for a Jewish state in Palestine in April 1945.[24] The newly elected Labour government, however, did not hear and attempted to prevent survivors from reaching Palestine at any cost – including sending boatloads of Jews back to Germany. Prime Minister Clement Atlee rejected President Truman's request to allow 100,000 Jews from displaced persons' camps in post-war Europe to leave for Palestine in 1945.

Moreover, Arab nationalists attacked Jewish communities throughout the Arab world. As early as 1941 a pogrom had taken place in Baghdad. In December 1947 the destruction of synagogues in Aleppo, in Syria, forced half the city's Jews to flee. In Egypt nearly 40% of the Jewish population had been forced to leave by 1950. In Algeria and Libya there were outbreaks of anti-Jewish violence.

All this made an indelible impression on Jews the world over and persuaded them to support the Zionist endeavour. Several thousand volunteers, mainly Jews, fought and died in Israel in 1948. Many understood this conflict as the possible next step in the genocidal war against the Jews. Left-wing non-Jews joined them – the American William Edmondson, the son of Irish immigrants, was killed on the road to Jerusalem in July 1948.[25]

A majority of Diaspora Jews today – even those who may disagree with the policies of an Israeli government – would probably regard support for the idea of a sovereign state of Israel as a fundamental pillar of their Jewish identity. The Jews are a nation and have a right to national self-determination. Other Jews – whether on the far Left or among the ultra-orthodox – would define themselves as anti-Zionist. While others who accept the fait accompli of the state of Israel would embrace the term 'non-Zionist'.

Many philo-Semitic non-Jews saw Zionism as a movement of affirmative action, the securing of a haven for the persecuted where Jews would no longer be history's scapegoat. Others, who were not so well disposed towards the Jews, were similarly delighted at the prospect of the departure of their Jewish population. Polish nationalists in the late 1930s were only too happy to support the evacuation plans of the Revisionist Zionists. Capturing the flavour of those times, the liberal Hungarian statesman Baron Eotvos once commented: 'An anti-semite is a man who dislikes the Jews more than he should.' To confuse things further, many non-Jews who sympathized with Zionist aspirations, such as David Lloyd-George and Aneurin Bevan, also styled themselves 'Zionists'. Bevan and the Old Left in Britain viewed Zionist colonization as a unique socialist experiment. Today in the United States many evangelicals identify themselves as Christian Zionists for specifically theological reasons. Many believe that the establishment of the state of Israel in 1948 and the capture of Jerusalem in 1967 were divinely inspired and herald the second coming of Jesus. There are even groups who believe themselves to be the 'lost Jewish tribes' in places as far apart as Zimbabwe and Papua New Guinea. They too use the term 'Zionist' to describe their affiliation to the Jewish people.

2

Who were the Zionists?

The End of Jewish History?

Zionism arose in Europe during the nineteenth century for two main reasons. First, a fragmentation of Jewish identity due to the *Haskalah* (Enlightenment) and the political legacy of the French Revolution; second, the rise of modern anti-Semitism in Europe as a result of the rise of the nation state, which inherited and transformed the traditional teachings of anti-Judaism within both Catholicism and Eastern Orthodoxy.

In revolutionary France in 1789 the condition of a reviled and despised people, walled up in their ghettos, became a potent symbol of a stultifying, repressive past – and their liberation a signpost on the road to change. The very existence of the Jews after centuries of persecution and degradation was a rejoinder to the popes and kings who had been the instruments of their attempted extinction. Remarkably the Jews managed to survive and chameleon-like had adapted to each new adverse situation. Yet when the Jews were indeed liberated it was as a badge of the new liberalism, according to the rationale of reason rather than to the reality of the Jewish situation – the reality of discrimination, impoverishment and persecution. If theory did not accommodate the Jews, it was easier to make the Jews accommodate theory. This, coupled with the pervasive idea that a nation state should be composed of a single nationality, left many Jews in a state of limbo. The revolutionary vision of France was one of a nation free of ethnicity – Jewish Frenchmen were welcome, but not French Jews. For a couple of generations such sophistication was lost on most Jews. No matter how good the intentions, by the end of the nineteenth century emancipation had failed. In a period of rising judeophobia, too many Jews discovered that they could no longer masquerade as bona fide French or Germans or Italians. Jews concluded that the answer to their predicament was self-emancipation rather than emancipation by others. There were several possibilities for a solution – universalist such as Bolshevism or particularist like the socialism of the Bund, or territorialist, espousing a specific land for settlement or non-territorialist, a Zion in Palestine or a Zion in another land – and subdivisions within and cross-fertilizations between them. One estimate suggested that there were twenty-two rival ideologies.[26] All competed for the allegiance of the Jews. One hundred years ago Zionism was just one choice among many.

The idea of a return to the Land of Israel had been emphasized by rabbinical scholars ever since the destruction of the Temple in Jerusalem in 70 CE. During the first war against the Romans, 66–70, the historian Josephus wrote that 115,880 bodies were carried through one city gate in a three-month period. Tacitus quotes a total figure of 600,000 dead during the siege of Jerusalem. The Emperor Vespasian and his son Titus set fire to a greater part of the city. Some who survived the onslaught were sold into slavery in marketplaces throughout the Roman Empire. Others served its fleet as galley slaves or worked in its mines. A revolt by Shimon Bar Kokhba between 132 and 135 was similarly crushed. Jerusalem was renamed Aelia Capitolina as a place of worship of Jupiter Capitolinus and the Emperor Hadrian decreed that no Jew should be allowed to enter its walls.

The idea of a Jewish national home did not vanish with its destruction. Instead, for the next eighteen centuries, the study of Jewish texts and the evolution of customs and traditions became a portable homeland for a marginalized and scattered people. The Talmud emerged as a compendium of statements, commentaries and interpretations for succeeding generations. The study of an accumulative body of scholarly discourse became the *raison d'être* for Jewish existence. Rabbis led their communities and, as *shtadlanim* (court Jews), often represented them to the authorities who governed their lives. From one generation to the next the wisdom of rabbinical teachings came to be understood as the worldly manifestation of divine inspiration.

Ahavat Tsion – the yearning for Zion – became a dormant but dominant theme for the Jews of the Diaspora. Jerusalem was not forgotten. In their thrice-daily prayers Jews referred to the Holy City and faced in its direction. Indeed the rabbis counted seventy names for Jerusalem in the Bible and one Talmudic commentator proudly proclaimed: 'Ten measures of beauty descended upon the world: Jerusalem took nine and the rest of the world one.'[27] Even for Jews who had never visited the Holy Land, the symbol of Jerusalem became ever more powerful in the imagination. Moreover, Jews continued to maintain a presence in the Holy Land throughout pre-Christian, Christian and Islamic rule.

Christianity became the religion of the Roman Empire in the fourth century. Its rise mirrored the catastrophe that had befallen the Jews – the loss of their Temple and the decimation of their homeland. This, the Church Fathers argued, was evidence that God had transferred his allegiance to the new Israel, that Christianity had superseded Judaism. An attempt by the Emperor Julian the Apostate (360–363) to reintroduce Hellenism and to allow the Jews to rebuild the Temple was extinguished by his successors. The concessions he made to the Jews, albeit temporarily, were deeply resented by the Christians. Such enmity extended from Rome in the West to Byzantine in the East. Jewish support for the Persian invasion of the Middle East in the seventh century resulted in a further expulsion of the Jews from Jerusalem by the Emperor Heraclius. Thus when Arab tribes from the Hejaz conquered Palestine, the Jews had already lost their central position. As under Byzantine rule, the land was divided into two and governed separately. Jerusalem fell in 637 to Omar and the success of the army of Islam brought with it a wave of Arab migration and colonization.

The Jerusalem of the Jewish imagination was not the Jerusalem of reality. Visitors throughout the ages testified to its utter desolation. Mark Twain wrote about a land in 'sackcloth and ashes' and described Jerusalem as 'a pauper village' after visiting the Holy Land in the nineteenth century. The outer western wall of the Temple precinct became known as the 'Wailing Wall' because of the ageless laments for destroyed Jerusalem.

Although Jews were generally well treated under Islamic rule, there were also periods when negative attitudes manifested themselves. Although both Jews and Christians were *dhimmi* (protected subjects), they were often subjected to a series of discriminatory laws accumulated over several centuries. They were allowed only to live in a specific locality and to wear yellow clothes and hats so as not to resemble Muslims in their mode of dress. Jewish houses and synagogues had to be lower than

Muslim houses and mosques. Jews were prohibited from carrying arms or owning slaves. In the eleventh century there were massacres of Jews in Fez and Granada. During the rule of the Mamluks synagogues throughout the Empire were closed between 1301 and 1310. Forced conversions took place in Baghdad in the fourteenth century and in Mashed, in Persia, as late as March 1839. All these measures were designed to enforce the lesser status of Jews in Islamic society.

But it was the resurgent Christianity of the European Crusades which brought death and destruction to many Jewish communities. The preaching of Peter the Hermit in Cologne on Easter Sunday in 1096 incited and enraged a growing army of his supporters. One Jewish source recorded:

> It came to pass on the tenth of Iyar, on Sunday, they plotted craftily against them. They took a trampled corpse of theirs, that had been buried thirty days previously and carried it through the city, saying: 'Behold what the Jews have done to our comrade. They took a gentile and boiled him in water. Then they poured the water into our wells in order to kill us.' When the crusaders and the burghers heard this, they cried out and gathered – all who bore and unsheathed (a sword) from great to small – saying: 'Behold the time has come to avenge him who was crucified, whom their ancestors slew. Now let not a remnant or a residue escape, even an infant or a suckling in the cradle.' They then came and struck those who had remained in their houses – comely young men and comely and lovely young women along with elders.[28]

The massacres committed during the religious fervour of the Crusades were not forgotten by the Jews, who commemorated the killings in prayer and poetry – mainly in the liturgy of Yom

Kippur. The desire to return to Jerusalem was expressed in their prayers and analyses of texts. While the physical Jerusalem became detached from the spiritual one evoked by prayer, this belief in return never left the Jews despite all their ordeals.

The Jews could depend only on the whims and favours of those who ruled them. More often than not they became pawns in power games between rival empires and competing religions. Thus while the Crusaders killed Jews, Saladin issued a proclamation to them to return and settle in Jerusalem. This initiated a wave of Jewish emigration from England and France in 1210. Two centuries later the Pope ordered Italian fleets not to carry Jews to the Holy Land. The treatment of Jews in medieval Christian Europe, however, always ensured emigration to Palestine. In Western Europe Jews who were expelled from the Spain of Ferdinand and Isabella in 1492 sought refuge in Safed in Palestine and developed it into a centre for Kabbalah. In 1548 it was noted that 716 out of 1900 tax-paying families in Safed were Jewish. Exactly a century later the Chmielnicki massacres of up to 100,000 Jews in the Ukraine brought another influx of Jews into Palestine.

Refuge and Persecution in Eastern Europe

Persecution and discrimination ensured that the Jews were always a people on the move. When there was a prospect of living in peace and harmony, they eagerly grasped it. Poland, the graveyard of modern Jewry as a result of the Holocaust, was such a land of opportunity some seven hundred years ago. The Mongol invasion in 1241 required a loyal bulwark to stop further incursions. The Polish princes wanted to expand and Polonize their border lands. The Polish–Lithuanian commonwealth thus became an area of successful Jewish settlement. Yet while Polish rulers welcomed their growing presence, the Church and local merchants bitterly opposed it. The former saw the Jews as a theologically corrupting influence while the latter did not wish them to have the same economic opportunities as Christians.

Vilna became a centre of Talmudic study and was popularly known as the Jerusalem of Lithuania. By the time of the French Revolution nearly 7% of the population of Poland were Jews, and in some of the larger towns they comprised half of the inhabitants. Poland, however, was devoured by its larger neighbours Russia, Prussia and Austria in a series of partitions and by 1795 had ceased to exist. Such aggrandizement had its price. For Russia, which had inherited the Byzantine Christian intolerance of Jews, the number of Jews within its new borders rose from under 1000 to well over 400,000. Catherine the Great, who ruled from 1762 to 1796, initiated a 'fencing-in' of these new human acquisitions in an area which became known as the 'Pale of Settlement' to prevent Jews – and particularly Jewish merchants – from settling in Russia.

Catherine's successors imposed further draconian measures on the Jews to decrease their numbers. Conversion was one method, conscription was another. Boys as young as twelve were taken for pre-military training and then at eighteen inducted into the military for twenty-five years. Each Jewish community had to supply a quota of conscripts. All this was designed to turn the community in on itself. The well-to-do and community leaders pulled every string to ensure that their sons escaped this fate. Instead the vulnerable and the poor became the scapegoats. Marauding bands of abductors were employed by the community to ensure that the quota was met. But even this became insufficient and eventually old men, cripples, invalids and even children under eight became soldiers of the Tsar.

Between 1649 and 1881 over 600 laws were passed by the Romanov dynasty to hem in and control the Jews – half of them promulgated during the reign of Nicholas I between 1825 and 1855. Jews were prevented from integrating into majority communities and could not take Russian first names. They could neither move out of the Pale of Settlement nor exercise even a modicum of self-government in the areas where they lived. Jews could neither do business on the Christian Sabbath and holidays nor conduct trade in Russia itself. Critical literary works which offended the political or religious sensibilities of the authorities were banned and sometimes burned publicly.

Such suppression – both physical and psychological – inspired Jews in Eastern Europe to dream of a better future. It also forced young Jews to question the good intentions of their rabbis and communal elders who appeared to acquiesce in the torment and passively accept all that was meted out by their oppressors. Although the situation improved initially under Alexander II, the 'Tsar-Liberator' (1855–81), Jews still endured great hardships under the weight of anti-Jewish legislature. By the late nineteenth century over half of the world's eight million Jews lived under Tsarist rule in conditions of great poverty and deprivation.

Education was a means of escaping the hopelessness of a wasted life. But in Russia universities were authorized to take a Jewish quota, often limited to 5% of candidates, regardless of ability. The better-off sent their sons abroad for an education. For Lithuanian Jews, Berlin was a favoured, nearby location. Graduates returned with a new way of looking at the world – through the eyes of the Enlightenment and the legacy of the French Revolution. The Tsarist regime attempted by every means possible to block the ideas of Kant and Voltaire from seeping in. But Kant's motto 'Dare to Know' was highly attractive to the thousands of Jewish students who were studying the Talmud and Torah at *yeshivot* (seminaries). Their training in the minutiae of discussion and the dissection of ideas prepared the ground for the new thinking to be absorbed with enthusiasm. The works of the eighteenth-century German-Jewish philosopher Moses Mendelssohn were particularly influential. He translated the Bible into German and in works such as *Jerusalem* (1783) and *Morning Hours* (1785) argued for a transformation of the older understanding of Judaism and God on a more rational basis. Similarly Gotthold Ephraim Lessing's play *Nathan the Wise* – a plea for religious tolerance – resonated within the world of the *yeshiva*.

In Western Europe, while broadening and secularizing Jewish identity, the *Haskalah* evolved into an essentially fragmenting and disintegrative process. The challenge of modernity promoted a plethora of Jewish identities and a series of interpretations of Judaism. It also brought the attractions of assimilation, acculturation and conversion. By contrast, in Eastern Europe the effects of the Berlin *Haskalah* were integrative. New thought patterns were merged into the traditional and a new type of Jewishness and Jewish culture began to evolve. In the closing years of the nineteenth century a transitional generation of Jewish intellectuals emerged who were educated in the *yeshiva* but drawn towards the world of modern thought and rational action. They could neither renounce past understanding of Judaism nor accept it.

The Zionist intelligentsia evolved from this milieu. Ahad Ha'am (One of the People) was the pseudonym of Asher Hirsch Ginsburg. His life was typical of this generation. Born into a family of Ruzhiner Hasidim, he moved through several ideological stages to become the progenitor of spiritual Zionism. An *ilui* (child prodigy) at the age of ten, he became the 'rebbe' of the growing circle of Zionist thinkers. Ahad Ha'am started with the teachings of the Sadegora Rebbe and Rabbi Israel Salanter's *Musar* movement and made the transition to the writings of Mendelssohn and the *maskilim* (Enlightenment scholars) of the Berlin *Haskalah*. He then began to devour the works of British philosophers – Bentham, Locke, Mill, Hume and Spencer. A follower of Ahad Ha'am was Chaim Nachman Bialik, who became the Hebrew national poet. He made a similar life journey from the *yeshiva* of Volozhin. The Hebrew writer Peretz Smolenskin joined the *yeshiva* of Shklov at the age of eleven and became a leading exponent of the *Haskalah* in editing the Hebrew literary periodical *Ha-Shachar*. Such figures began life in the black garments of the ultra-orthodox in Tsarist Russia and grew old in the Land of Israel in conventional European dress.

In the wake of the French Revolution a Jewish cultural intelligentsia developed mainly in Western Europe around the idea of the *Wissenschaft Des Judentums* (the science of Judaism), which examined Judaism through modern methods of research, biblical criticism and analysis. It constructed a wider understanding of the Jewish experience to embrace Jewish literature and culture as well as Judaism itself and religious philosophy. Jewish history – rather than the history of Judaism – was being reclaimed. Isaac Jost published the first history of the Jews in the 1820s. As if to break with the theologically driven past, he wrote: 'No prejudice should bind the historian; no universally held dogma should darken his views; no apprehension should intimidate him from revealing the truth as he sees it. He must be able to look around freely, to examine clearly the subjects of his field, to illumine the dark, to bring out what is hidden. Anyone who might take offence at this should retreat into the darkness and refresh himself in indolent slumber.'[29]

Solomon Rapoport, later the Chief Rabbi of Prague, wrote several biographical studies of medieval religious leaders such as Saadia Gaon and Eleazar ha-Kallir and applied a new critical approach to rabbinic history. Nachman Krochmal posited a new philosophy of Jewish history. The Jews, he argued, were like every other nation, with periods of birth, development, ascendancy and decline. Yet the Jews were also different – they were an eternal people and unlike other peoples did not make a transient appearance in history and then disappear. The basis of this eternity was God's unending relationship with the Jews: not so much a chosen people, but one selected by God for special tasks.

It was Heinrich Graetz, through the publication of his eleven-volume *History of the Jews* between 1853 and 1876, who introduced both Western European Jews and non-Jews to the idea that the Jews were an ancient national group which had survived the battering of millennia. The flourishing of such writing lent weight to the idea that there was more to the history of the Jewish people than the history of Judaism and its rabbinical figures. The *Wissenschaft Des Judentums* effectively transformed Judaic history into Jewish history. In so doing, it projected the idea of a Jewish civilization, often with Judaism at its core, but encompassing history, literature, languages and culture.

Such changes excited many Jews, but conservative non-Jews viewed this as a dangerous development. When the Society for the Enlightenment of the Jews in Odessa started to publish Graetz's history in Russian translation, the ecclesiastical censor in St Petersburg banned the work as 'an irreverent treatment of sacred history'. The Holy Synod of the Russian Orthodox Church examined the manuscript and decided that all existing copies of the book should be burned.[30]

The writing of Jewish history reclaimed the past and gave the Jews an understanding of who they were and where they came from. Their place in history as builders of a Jewish civilization – albeit dispersed and multicultural – was a catalyst for new intellectual initiatives, particularly during the 1860s, the liberal period of Alexander II. A plethora of periodicals appeared which addressed the pertinent questions of the day. These publications appeared in three languages. This was not surprising since the Jews were always a trilingual people. During the period of the Second Temple and King Herod, Jews used Greek as the general language of the region to converse, Aramaic between themselves and Hebrew, 'the holy language', for prayer and scholarly study.

Two thousand years later in Tsarist Russia the pattern was repeated. Most of the publications were in Yiddish, the language of the Jewish masses of Eastern Europe, and included titles such as *Kol Mevasser* (The Voice of the Messenger), which appeared in 1862. There were the Russifiers such as Leon Pinsker who believed that the Russian language and culture would shape the Jewish future: hence the appearance of *Rassvet* (Dawn) in 1860 and the weekly *Den* (The Day) in 1869. But what broke the mould was the appearance of periodicals in Hebrew. It was no longer solely a language associated with prayer and the synagogue, but one in which the intellectual issues of the day were dissected. It had been reclaimed as a language for discourse by former *yeshiva* students. Hebrew remained 'the holy language', but such an appellation was now being stretched to investigate literature, culture, history, poetry and the workings of the Jewish Diaspora.

The reclamation of Hebrew as 'a living language' began with Mendelssohn and the Berlin *Haskalah*. The German *maskilim* used the Hebrew term '*Haskalah*' rather than the German

'*Aufklärung*' to describe the Jewish Enlightenment. Although Yiddish was essentially the language of the Jews, it was regarded – by both Westernized Jews and non-Jews – as a debased form of German; more an illiterate jargon than a language of elegance. Hebrew, however, evoked a glorious past and was elevated through the prestige of the Bible. It was also the written language of educated Jews. For the German *maskilim*, it symbolized enlightenment, education and reason.

In one sense the reclamation of Hebrew was a revolt against the ignorance and superstition of the Jewish masses. The first Hebrew periodical, *Ha-Me'assef*, appeared in Königsberg in 1784 as a vehicle for the views of the Berlin *maskilim*. This recast Moses as a rationalist figure in the image of the *Haskalah* in Naphtali Hirz Wessely's epic poem *Shirei Tiferet* (Poems of Splendour). But the Berlin *Haskalah* may have had a totally different reason for using Hebrew. It can be argued that the reclamation of Hebrew in Germany was merely a staging post on the road to using the German language and absorbing German culture. After all, Mendelssohn spoke of 'we Germans'.

In Eastern Europe the *Haskalah* and the use of Hebrew had a totally different effect. In Russia the periodical *Ha-Melitz* (The Advocate) appeared in Odessa in 1860 under the editorship of Alexander Tsederbaum. This served as the central repository for the works of the best-known Hebrew writers, both in Russia and abroad. *Ha-Shachar* (The Dawn) appeared in Vienna a few years later, edited by Peretz Smolenskin. It became the standard-bearer of the radical elements of the *Haskalah* – hence it was printed abroad and taken across the border. Smolenskin railed not only against religious obscurantism, but also against assimilation and acculturation. The monthly served as an organ of cultural nationalism. It was much more than simply literary entertainment in a reclaimed language.

Smolenskin ensured that Eastern Europe did not follow the path of emancipated Western Europe. Writers such as Judah Leib Gordon developed this trend in such poems as 'Awake, My People'. Gordon attacked the spiritualization of Jewish history at the expense of its national character. This explains his sympathetic treatment of Zedekiah, the last King of Judah, whose rebellion against the Babylonian Nebuchadnezzar led to the destruction of the First Temple. Zedekiah was normally castigated as weak and vacillating in the Bible, but in Gordon's Hebrew poem 'Zedekiah in Prison', the king is used to criticize the spiritual unworldliness of the prophet Jeremiah – clearly a metaphor for rabbinical authority in Tsarist Russia.

Through his periodical Smolenskin attempted to develop a cultural nationalism for a people who were rapidly beginning to see themselves as an ethnic minority rather than simply as an isolated, marginalized religious group that was neither Christian nor Muslim. Indeed the Jews became a nation in the modern sense in nineteenth-century Tsarist Russia – and particularly in the concentrated and hermetically sealed Pale of Settlement. It was in Eastern Europe that they became more than the People of the Book.

'Who are We?'

The nineteenth century can be seen as decisive for the Jews of Eastern Europe in their transition from a religious Judaic identity to a national Jewish one, from passivity to activism, from conservatism to radicalism. The situation of the Jews was grave. Many possibilities were open to them – emigration to the New World, revolutionary universalism, a territory in Argentina where they could transform themselves into gauchos; conversion to Christianity, whether Catholicism or Protestantism. Zionism and the emigration of Jews to Palestine was merely one solution considered by the Jewish intelligentsia. For many Jews, it seemed utopian and unworkable – the harbinger of a difficult life. Up until 1881 emigration to the holy cities of Jerusalem, Safed, Tiberias and Hebron was the prerogative of the pious, who led a poverty-stricken life of study and devotion and depended on the donations of their brethren abroad to keep them and their families afloat.

In 1881 Tsar Alexander II was assassinated by the revolutionary organization *Narodnaya Volia* (The People's Will), which demanded the establishment of a Constituent Assembly as the precondition for renouncing violence. His successor, Alexander III (1881–94), was carried to his throne on a wave of slavophilism and reaction. Russia moved to the nationalist Right. Jews were branded as liberals, revolutionaries and subversives, as well as Christ-killers. This escalated into a series of pogroms across the Empire, often under the less-than-watchful eyes of the police. Laws passed between the summer of 1881 and May 1882 were designed to punish the Jews in every way possible. They were now no longer welcome to even settle in the Pale of Settlement – an area of one million square kilometres stretching from the Baltic Sea in the north to the Black Sea in the south. The definition of 'new visitors' to a village or town was interpreted arbitrarily, with the result that tens of thousands of Jews were forced to leave their homes and driven into the cities. The impetus often came from Russian members of a particular village who were formally given the right by the authorities to drive out those deemed unsavoury, hostile and simply different. The quota for Jews at institutes of higher education was reduced even further, and the same happened in the professions.

Such measures heralded the end of the Pale of Settlement. It disrupted the concentration of Jews gathered there and redistributed them. Many fled to the slums of the nearest city and became urbanized. Others emigrated to America, Britain and South Africa. In 1870–71 just over 1000 emigrated from Russia to the United States. In 1881–2, the figure jumped to 17,497. During the year of expulsions from many Russian cities, 1891–2, it increased to 76,417. In the year of the Kishinev pogrom, 1903–04, 77,544 left for the New World. While large numbers of Jews sought their salvation outside Russia, a few began to think about Palestine. At the beginning of 1882 Jewish students formed a group called BILU. This was the Hebrew acronym for a quote from the Book of Isaiah: 'O House of Jacob, come and let us go.'[31] The first group of fourteen immigrants reached Jaffa in July 1882.

The pogroms of 1881 and the discriminatory May Laws particularly affected those Jews who believed that Russification was the solution to the Jewish problem. The new legislation, for example, prohibited Jews from trading on Sundays and on Christian holidays as well as forcing them to settle outside major towns. The new Tsar's policies had made it clear that Jews would be neither assimilated nor absorbed into the Russian people. They were unwanted. Chaim Hisin, one of the first of the BILU immigrants, wrote in his diary:

The recent pogroms have violently awakened the complacent Jews from their sweet slumbers. Until now, I was uninterested in my origin. I saw myself as a faithful son of Russia which was to me my raison d'être and the very air that I breathed. Each new discovery by a Russian scientist, every classical literary work, every victory of the Russian Empire would fill my heart with pride. I wanted to devote my whole strength to the good of my homeland, and happily do my duty. Suddenly they come and show us the door and openly declare that we are free to leave for the West.[32]

This policy of excluding Jews from Russian society affected Leon Pinsker. His father had been a *maskil* and he himself served honourably as a doctor in the Crimean War. In the liberal period of the 1860s Pinsker was involved in founding several Russian-language Jewish periodicals and was active in the Odessa branch of the Society for the Enlightenment of the Jews.

Like other Russifiers, he was profoundly shocked at the outbreak of violence in 1881. The pogroms started in the town of Yelizavetgrad in April and then spread to other hamlets and villages in the Ukraine, which had a history of violence against Jewish communities stretching back to the Chmielnicki massacres of 1648. Attacks on Jews followed soon after in cities such as Kiev, Odessa and Dneipropetrovsk, which soon bore witness to rape, looting and the destruction of property. During the summer of 1882 the wave of pogroms spread to Poland, Belarus and Lithuania and the murder of whole families was not uncommon. In many places the authorities were either indifferent or slow to react. Often the local peasantry would vent their religious wrath against the alleged killers of Christ. The pogrom in Balta at Easter 1882 resulted in the killing of many Jews and the injuring of over 100, the pillage of over 1200 homes and shops and the rape of many young women.

Leon Trotsky, the founder of the Red Army, was born Lev Davidovich Bronstein and made a determined attempt to marginalize his Jewishness. Yet he could not forget the fear of the pogrom of his Jewish background. Trotsky wrote about the almost festive preparations for a pogrom in 1905:

Proclamations calling for a pogrom are disseminated, blood-thirsty articles appear in Provincial News, sometimes a special newspaper starts to appear. The governor of Odessa issues in his name a provocative proclamation. When the way is paved, there then appear the actors, experts in their job. In their wake there circulate . . . ominous rumours: the Jews are gathering to attack the Greek Orthodox; the socialists have desecrated the sacred icons; the students have torn the tsar's portrait . . . blacklists of people and lodgings marked for destruction in the first wave are drawn up. . . On the appointed day a public prayer is held in church. A priest delivers a solemn address. A patriotic procession takes place led by members of the clergy, carrying the Tsar's portrait, controlled by the police, with plenty of flags. The band continuously plays martial music.[33]

The events of 1881 and 1882 profoundly affected Pinsker and he attempted to discuss the choices facing Russian Jewry with several prominent European Jews. It was the President of the Board of Deputies of British Jews, Arthur Cohen MP, who suggested that he should write about his misgivings. Pinsker's pamphlet *Auto-Emancipation* appeared in 1882. He argued that emancipation by others – as envisaged by the Enlightenment and the French Revolution – was a pipe dream. The Jews had to emancipate themselves through the establishment of a Jewish national home.

The reactionaries, he argued, wished to eliminate their Jews through violence and discrimination. The revolutionaries wished the Jews to cease to exist through assimilation. For the former, the Jewish people were seen as an international cabal bent on corroding Holy Russia. For the latter, the Jews were not a people at all since their very existence was a pure anomaly, a quirk of history – and their contribution to history's advance should be their disappearance. In his pamphlet Pinsker argued that the Jews were an object of both hatred and puzzlement for the nations among whom they lived:

> This ghostly apparition of a people without unity or organization, without land or other bond of union, no longer alive, and yet moving among the living – this eerie form scarcely paralleled in history, unlike anything that preceded or followed it, could not fail to make a strange and peculiar impression upon the imagination of the nations. And if the fear of ghosts is something inborn, and has a certain justification in the psychic life of humanity, is it any wonder that it asserted itself so powerfully at the sight of this dead and yet living nation?[34]

Pinsker pointed to the rise of anti-Semitism as a consequence of the advent of the nation state in nineteenth-century Europe. In some countries Jews were less expendable than in others, but in all they were viewed as foreigners and outsiders, not as loyal citizens of the Jewish faith. In the worst cases they were seen as a serious threat to the host nation because they were perceived to be in economic competition with the rest of the population. At the age of sixty Pinsker turned his back on his previous belief of embracing Russian culture. Now his solution was a territorialist one – a country where Jews could determine their own fate.

The pogroms were psychologically devastating to the Jewish intelligentsia who had placed their hopes in a liberal Russia. One wrote: 'My heart is filled with corroding despair from which there is no escape. This terrible insult flung at us is destroying me. It seems to me that even if I succeeded in settling in a country where all were equal and where no lootings, no Jewish committees existed, I would still remain spiritually crushed to the end of my days.'[35]

There was also a deep degree of remorse and self-examination. Jewish intellectuals' acceptance of Russification and their semi-assimilation produced hand-wringing by the idea's former devotees:

> The 'enlightened' Jews had repudiated their history, forgotten their traditions, and come to despise everything that made them conscious of belonging to an eternal people. Without an intelligent understanding of Jewish ideals and burdened by Judaism even as an escaped convict is hampered by heavy chains, what could compensate for their belonging to a tribe of 'Christ-killers' and 'exploiters'? How pathetic is the position of those who advocated fusion with the Russian people through national self-abnegation. Life and the logic of events demand that the Jew define his position, for it has become impossible to occupy a seat between two chairs. Either one openly declares oneself a renegade or one decides to share the sufferings of his people.[36]

Jews who had joined the revolutionary movement were astounded when *Narodnaya Volia* called upon the peasants to join the instigators of the pogroms. In an address to the Ukrainian people by the executive committee on 30 August 1881, it stated: 'The damned police beat you, the landowners devour you, the Yids, the dirty Judases rob you. People in the Ukraine suffer most from the Yids. Who has seized the land, woodlands, the taverns? The Yids. Whom does the peasant beg with tears in his eyes to let him near his land? The Yids. Wherever you look, whatever you touch, everywhere the Yids. The Yid curses the peasant, cheats him, drinks his blood. The Yids make life unbearable.'[37]

When Pavel Axelrod, later a leading Menshevik, wished to respond to *Narodnaya Volia* by publishing a pamphlet entitled

On the Tasks of the Jewish Socialist Intelligentsia, Pyotr Lavrov, a leading theorist of populism at that time, argued that it was inexpedient to do so.[38] Few from the liberal intelligentsia and the revolutionary Left were willing to risk their contacts with 'the people' and unequivocally condemn the violent anti-Semitism. The writer Maxim Gorky, who had witnessed the Nizhni-Novgorod pogrom of July 1884, was a rare voice of protest. Many Russian intellectuals were so focused on their life-and-death struggle with the forces of reaction that the plight of the Jews was of lesser concern. Both Tolstoy and Turgenev, for example, remained silent during this period.

Former *yeshiva* teachers such as Moses Leib Lilienblum who had lost their faith and become adherents of Russian thinkers once more began to evaluate their spiritual and ideological journey. In an article of 1883 entitled 'The Future of Our People' Lilienblum delineated the hopelessness of the Jewish predicament:

> The opponents of nationalism see us as uncompromising nationalists, with a nationalist God and a nationalist Torah; the nationalists see us as cosmopolitans, whose homeland is wherever we happen to be well off. Religious gentiles say that we are devoid of any faith, and the freethinkers among them say that we are orthodox and believe in all kinds of nonsense; the liberals say we are conservative and the conservatives call us liberal. Some bureaucrats and writers see us as the root of anarchy, insurrection and revolt, and the anarchists say we are capitalists, the bearers of the biblical civilisation, which is, in their view, based on slavery and parasitism. Officialdom accuses us of circumventing the laws of the land – that is, of course, the laws directed specifically against us. . . Musicians like Richard Wagner charge us with destroying the beauty and purity of

music. Even our merits are turned into shortcomings: "Few Jews are murderers", they say, "because Jews are cowards." This, however, does not prevent them from accusing us of murdering Christian children.[39]

The pogroms of 1881 and the draconian measures of the new Tsarist regime concentrated the minds of the Jewish intelligentsia. Various solutions were put forward. It is significant that those who opted for a territorialist solution in Palestine, a resurrection of Zion, came from a wide variety of ideological directions – the Russifiers, the alienated, the assimilated, the revolutionaries, the liberals and the cultural nationalists. Events had moved them all from long-held views and unified them in praise of Zionism as the solution to the present. Above all, they shared a desire to regenerate the Jews as a people who could lead a national life and who would defend themselves. Peretz Smolenskin, the cultural nationalist, who had foreseen the pogroms, argued that the only salvation of the Jews lay in their own hands. It meant a turning away from a European past of desolation and looking towards the Land of Israel.

Why are we treated like this? Because we have sunk so low that our self-respect has died – because we have come to like charity flung at us in disgrace and contempt.

We have no sense of national honour; our standards are those of second class people. We find ourselves rejoicing when we are granted a favour and exulting when we are tolerated and befriended. Jewish writers sing aloud for joy when a Jew happens to be honoured. They do not tire of praising the graciousness of this or that gentile who overcomes his pride and makes some slight gesture towards a Jew. Alas for such kindness and tolerance and alas for our writers, poets and speakers who praise them. What is the real sadness of our estate? It is not the woes inflicted on us by our enemies but the wounds caused by our own brethren. If we really want to help the victims of the pogroms, we must proclaim unceasingly that we ourselves are responsible for our own inner weakness. We must turn from the path of disaster we once chose, for we can still be saved. Even at this late hour perhaps light can still come.[40]

Smolenskin understood that Zionism meant a revolution in Jewish life. It meant transforming both the Jews and the very idea of Jewishness.

The Experience in Western Europe

Jews in Western Europe also found their way to Zionism, not so much through a desire to create a Jewish renaissance, but as a reaction to growing anti-Semitism. If in the first half of the nineteenth century European nationalism had been a progressive internationalist force, by the 1880s the era of imperialism and ethnic superiority had begun. The German states in particular had coalesced into a confederation under Prussian hegemony. In Austro-Hungary, an evolving multi-ethnic empire, Jews had migrated from Czechoslovakia, Hungary and Polish Galicia to Vienna, where in the course of one generation they moved from extreme poverty to the comfort of the professional middle class. The Jewish population of Vienna had increased dramatically from 40,000 in 1869 to 120,000 in 1890. Their offspring took advantage of the opportunities at hand; for example, 48% of all medical students in Vienna in 1889 were Jewish.

Many from this second generation were removed from their

Jewish origins. Most were acculturated and some even converted. Liberal German nationalism was a beacon of enlightenment for Jews such as Freud, Mahler, Schnitzler and Alfred Adler. Yet as the century closed, the rise of anti-Semitism in Germany and Austria made this light grow progressively dim. Even France, to whose revolutionary banner Jews had rallied in the past – and which was still held in great esteem – was infected by this virus. At the end of December 1894 the closed trial for treason of Alfred Dreyfus, the first Jew to serve on the General Staff of the French Army, took place. Despite the transparency of a show trial on charges of passing documents to the Germans, Dreyfus remarkably demonstrated his allegiance by calling out 'Vive la France'. But in the age of empire even the most assimilated Jew was still considered to have a subversive agenda. As more facts came to light, many categorically refused to accept that a miscarriage of justice had taken place. The French Prime Minister attempted a cover-up while officers of the General Staff threatened to resign if Dreyfus was released from his cell on Devil's Island. In 1898 Émile Zola's famous open letter *J'accuse* in defence of Dreyfus was published. It created an intense debate, yet he was convicted for libel because of it. There were even anti-Jewish riots against any rehabilitation of Dreyfus. Although Dreyfus eventually found justice and was reinstated, Jews across Europe began to feel a rising tide of racism directed against them. If it could happen to an assimilated Jew such as Dreyfus, it was reasoned, assimilation was no defence against anti-Semitism. If it could happen in enlightened France, the historic epicentre of and inspiration for the European Revolutions, it could happen anywhere.

Theodor Herzl, the founder of the modern Zionist movement, grew to adulthood in such a milieu in Budapest and Vienna. Like Dreyfus, he embraced assimilationism enthusiastically and distanced himself from any vestige of Jewishness.

Moreover, he much appreciated the style of the new German nationalism and its agenda of heroic deeds, self-sacrifice and clear leadership. He adored the nobility of the aristocracy and detested the vulgarity of the bourgeoisie – and in particular the ostentatious nouveau riche, many of whom were second-generation Jews. Herzl regarded the Jews as a deformed people, thoroughly un-European and profoundly Asiatic. The German statesman and writer Walter Rathenau adopted similar views in calling for assimilation in his essay 'Höre, Israel!' in 1897. Accurately if somewhat inadvertently, he described such Jews in transition as 'a people of fear'.

Despite his convictions, the situation in *fin de siècle* Vienna forced Herzl to confront rising anti-Semitism. As a journalist and writer he observed the growing muteness of both liberal politicians and intellectuals. He realized that he could not escape his Jewish identity even if he wished to. His solution to the Jewish problem was initially conversion and intermarriage. Yet his disdain for Jewishness – and his ambivalence about his background – came at a time when political parties such as the Christian Social Party, who regarded Jews and liberals as one and the same, were in the ascendancy. They believed in 'Catholic values' and demanded that Jews be barred from teaching Christian children. Jews, they argued, should be excluded from the University of Vienna, which should be a purely Catholic institution. In parliament there was even a discussion about whether Christ should be considered a Jew.

Herzl worked as a journalist for the Viennese daily *Neue Freie Presse* and daily came across this growing judeophobia. He had read Eugen Karl Dühring's *The Jewish Question as a Question of Race, Morality and Culture*, which demanded the exclusion of Jews from public life. On a personal level all this created inner turmoil for Herzl. He considered himself neither a Magyar nor a Jew but an adherent of liberal German nation-alism. Yet he began to realize that he had no choice in the matter. The gatekeepers were now permitting only restricted entry to Viennese society. Given the city's new anti-Semitic cli-mate, he would have even found it difficult to enrol in his own university fraternity. How then could one adjust one's Jewishness to make Jews acceptable to the Viennese? In January 1893 Herzl wrote a letter to Vienna's Defence Association Against Anti-Semitism in which he suggested that anti-Semitism could not be fought by words but only by mass conversion to Christianity. He therefore proposed a mass bap-tism at St Stephen's Cathedral in the city.

The sense of isolation and of betrayal, especially by fair-weather liberals, forced Herzl to look deeper into himself. In 1893 a Viennese priest published a book which claimed to demonstrate conclusively that a murder of a young Christian some 400 years earlier had been the work of pious Jews follow-ing the dictates of religious teachings. The charges of such a blood libel, often repeated in many locations throughout the centuries, were disseminated widely and embellished in the press. Instead of prosecuting the priest, liberal politicians demurred at moving against someone in holy orders at a time of heightened anti-Semitism.

In 1894 Herzl began to write a play, *The New Ghetto*, which dissected the flaws of assimilation as a solution to the Jewish problem. He also discovered the glory of the Jewish past – real and imagined – and concluded that the 'deformed nature' of the Jewish people had been caused by its dispersion over the centuries. In early 1895 Karl Lüeger secured a narrow victory for the Christian Socials in the municipal elections in Vienna. It was probably this watershed amid his growing awareness and unease that propelled Herzl to write *The Jewish State*. This small pamphlet electrified Jews across Europe with a vision of the future, but particularly among the downtrodden masses of Eastern Europe. It argued that anti-Semitism showed no sign of fading away and assimilation was no protection. Jews would still be considered as aliens in the societies in which they lived – no matter how much they contributed to it. Religious antagonism, economic rivalry and social difference would worsen – and the Jews would suffer. The solution, Herzl maintained, was mass emigration and settlement in a new land where a Jewish state could be established.

Within a couple of years he had founded the Zionist Organization and arranged its first congress. Yet Herzl remained who he was – a Central European assimilated Jew who loved Wagner but had never read Ahad Ha'am, Pinsker or Bialik and regarded Eastern European Jews as backward. Therefore his *The Jewish State* was more a work for the semi-assimilated masses of Central and Western Europe. Among the nationally conscious masses of Eastern Europe the reaction was very different. Chaim Weizmann, the first President of Israel, noted in his autobiography:

We had never heard the name Herzl before; or perhaps it had come to our attention, only to be lost among those of other journalists and feuilletonists. Fundamentally *The Jewish State* contained not a single new idea for us; that which so startled the Jewish bourgeoisie, and called down the resentment and derision of the Western rabbis, had long been the substance of Zionist tradition. We observed too, that this man Herzl made no allusion in his little book to his predecessors in the field, to Moses Hess and Leon Pinsker and Nathan Birnbaum – the last a Viennese like Herzl and the creator of the very word by which the movement is known – Zionism.[41]

Weizmann went on to castigate Herzl for mentioning neither Palestine nor the Hebrew language. Indeed the German title of his work, *Der Judenstaat*, should really be translated as 'The State of the Jews' and not *The Jewish State*. As Ahad Ha'am commented, a Jewish state was different from a state of the Jews. It implied something new, something different, connected to the past and tradition – and not a state like any other. Herzl saw Jewish evacuation from Europe as an act of liberation for both Jews and non-Jews. He wanted the immediate establishment of a Jewish state which would precede the formation of a national movement. This immediately led to conflict with Eastern European Jewry, which had been influenced by Russian populism. The state, he proposed, would shape the nation and transform the Jews.

Ahad Ha'am viewed the *raison d'être* of Zionism as the establishment of a spiritual centre to which all Diaspora Jews would turn their heads: 'A national spiritual centre of Judaism to which all Jews will turn with affection, and which will bind all Jews together; a centre of study and learning, of language and literature, of bodily work and spiritual purification; a true miniature of the people of Israel as it ought to be.'[42]

The Jewish state, he argued, would eventually be established at an appropriate point in the distant future. Viennese Jews were aghast at Herzl's suggestions. Jewish editors on *Neue Freie Presse* were acutely embarrassed and no mention of *The Jewish State* ever appeared in its pages. The Jewish satirist Karl Kraus, who converted to Catholicism, blamed the Jews themselves for the rise of anti-Semitism and virulently condemned Zionism in publications such as *Eine Krone für Zion* (A Crown for Zion) of 1898.

Herzl became distrustful of France and its democratic traditions after working there as a journalist. Édouard-Adolphe

Drumont had published the racist *La France Juive* (Jewish France) in 1886. Herzl was keen on the idea of a monarch and saw the new state as 'a part of civilization – we don't want a Boer state, but a Venice'. Hebrew was to be discarded for German and a new Jewish Academy would be modelled on the French template. The new Zionist flag displayed seven stars on a white background, but no Jewish symbol. The seven stars represented the seven hours of the working day. The white background, Herzl proclaimed, was emblematic of the 'new and pure life' that Zionism promised. He had clearly been totally oblivious of the efforts of the Eastern Europeans. This and his Jewish illiteracy did not impress. Yet Herzl understood how to manage a squabbling band of proto-nationalists and how to promote Zionism to the Jewish masses. He understood how to exploit negative stereotypes of Jews which recognized neither authority nor borders, to pander to the prejudices of the rulers of Europe. Herzl put Zionism on the map through public advocacy and public relations. When he died at the age of forty-four in 1904, thousands of Jews across Europe sat *shiva* (the traditional seven days of mourning) for him.

If Herzl was the original Viennese Jewish liberal, his broad, distinctly apolitical General Zionism was a unifying force in name only. Factions within the movement swiftly began to emerge. But the seeds had been planted long before Herzl's appearance on the Zionist stage. Moses Hess, who had died twenty years before the publication of *The Jewish State*, was a colleague of Marx, and perhaps the first Socialist Zionist. As Isaiah Berlin commented, 'Moses Hess was both a communist and a Zionist. He played a decisive role in the history of the first movement; he virtually invented the second.'[43] Indeed Marx's seemingly disparaging comments about Jews in *Zur Judenfrage* (On the Jewish Question) have been traditionally interpreted as anti-Semitic rather than ironic – a riposte to the radical Bruno Bauer's authentic anti-Semitism.[44] Even so, Marx was influenced by Hess's adolescent criticisms of Jews and Jewishness.

Both Marx and Hess were part of that generation of Rhineland Jews who grew up under the egalitarianism of the French tricolour, only to see the Prussians later remove legislation which gave Jews opportunities in life. After Waterloo civil servants, teachers and lawyers who happened to be Jews were turned out of their jobs. Their return to their professional status could be paid for only in the currency of conversion and self-abasement. Heschel Halevi Marx was the son of the Chief Rabbi of Trier, a lawyer and a supporter of the Enlightenment who admired Voltaire. He became Heinrich Marx and converted to Protestantism. He then ensured that his son, Karl, had not even a distant memory of his Jewish background. The adult Karl Marx reinforced this excision by ruthlessly divesting himself of even the most rudimentary identification with Jews. Hess, however, was educated by his grandfather, the Chief Rabbi of Mannheim, and retained a deep sense of Jewishness throughout his life. In his *A Sacred History of Mankind* of 1837, Hess called for the socialist transformation of society. For Hess, Judaism was the embodiment of the spirit of solidarity. He believed in a socialist commonwealth in Palestine and public ownership of the land. Christianity, he argued, had produced individualistic capitalism whereas Judaism was based on a collectivity and a social ethos. Moreover, Hess was significantly not a young Hegelian like Marx and Engels and many other early socialists, but a follower of the rationalist Jewish philosopher Baruch Spinoza.

Spinoza postulated a rational history of God as opposed to the abstract spirituality of Christianity. He was expelled by the Jewish community of Amsterdam in 1656 and in 1670 published his famous *Tractatus Theologico-Politicus* on biblical criticism. Hess argued that Spinoza's ideas laid the foundations for both the American and French Revolutions. Unlike the young Hegelians, Hess was not enamoured with the epoch of terror under Robespierre in revolutionary France and did not accept that the German spirit alone would redeem humankind. In his essay on the Socialist Zionist Hess, Isaiah Berlin remarks:

> Marx genuinely believed that what alone made a cause worth fighting for was that it represented the inevitable next stage in the social evolution of men as rational beings, a stage that could be determined accurately only by means of scientific analysis and prediction. . . Hess believed that social equality was desirable because it was just, not because it was inevitable; nor was justice to be identified with whatever was bound, in any case from the womb of time. All kinds of bad and irrational conditions had been produced before now, and persisted. Nothing was to be accepted merely because it had occurred – but solely because it was objectively good.[45]

In his *Rome and Jerusalem*, published in 1862, just after the reunification of Italy, Hess argued that if the Jews were to contribute to the advance of humanity, they must first extricate themselves from the ravages of identity-less acculturation in Western Europe and the obscurantism of orthodox leadership in Eastern Europe. Palestine, he suggested, would become the destination for Jewish emigrants, and he called upon France, the liberator of nations, to help them move from slavery to freedom.

Hess's Zionism was universalist – and while others looked to the liberation of Italy as symbolic, he looked to the liberation of the Land of Israel:

I believe that not only does the national essence of Judaism not exclude civilisation and humanitarianism, but that the latter really follow from it, as necessarily as the result follows from the cause. . . There is not a phase in Christian morality, nor in the scholastic philosophy of the Middle Ages, nor in modern philanthropy, and, if we add the latest manifestation of Judaism, Spinozism, not even in modern philosophy, which does not have its roots in Judaism. Until the French Revolution, the Jewish people was the only people in the world which had, simultaneously, a national as well as a humanitarian religion. It is through Judaism that the history of humanity has become a sacred history.[46]

3

What did Zionism Teach?

A Plethora of Zionisms

Zionism was never a monolithic movement. It would be more correct to speak of a range of different varieties of Zionism. Herzl's General Zionism immediately began to flow into different ideological streams. There was the Marxist Zionism of Dov Ber Borochov and the first kibbutzniks. Indeed they viewed themselves as the Zionist wing of the Russian revolutionary movement. Others rejected ideological straightjackets and plumped for the Tolstoyan self-dignity of A. D. Gordon and the land cultivators. Rabbis such as Yitzhak Reines and Meir Bar-Ilan established the Religious Zionist movement because they believed that the mainstream movement would eliminate Judaism from the teaching and activities of Zionism. Hence their slogan 'The Land of Israel for the People of Israel according to the Torah of Israel'. Labour Zionists such as David Ben-Gurion and Yitzhak Ben-Zvi set out to build and control a Zionist economy and to shape a workers' society. The Histadrut – the General Confederation of Hebrew Labour in the Land of Israel – was founded in 1920 and uniquely performed the functions of both employer and employee. It facilitated the proliferation and development of kibbutzim, established healthcare for all workers and even determined the length of the working day.

Vladimir Jabotinsky, representing the nationalists, on the other hand, was proud to entitle an article 'We, the Bourgeoisie' in the late 1920s. He argued that socialism stifled human initiative and individualism. He had grown tired of the lack of progress during the 1920s and broke with Weizmann's plodding diplomacy. Inspired by the European national movements of the early nineteenth century, Jabotinsky propagated a red-blooded Zionism which attracted many young people in Eastern Europe. He did not conceal Zionist desires for a state and called for it to be built on both sides of the River Jordan – on the East Bank and the West Bank. Even Herzl's inheritors of non-factional Zionism proclaimed themselves to be a non-party party – the General Zionists. Yet they too split into General Zionists 'A' and General Zionists 'B'.

Nachman Syrkin provided the first dissent within the newly established Zionist movement. He publicly attacked the liberal Herzl for his utopianism and his romanticism. Writing in May 1901, Syrkin commented:

The reactionary bourgeois character of modern Zionism has discredited the conception of the Jewish renaissance in the eyes of Jewish socialists. However – the mistaken belief of some socialists to the contrary – Zionism does not spring from the desire of the Jewish middle class to find new spheres for capitalist exploitation. Such an explanation of this remarkable movement is crude and naïve. Zionism springs from the consciousness of the Jewish masses that their economic positions have been shattered and from their desire for a more tolerable way of life.[47]

Like Hess, Syrkin argued that there were no fixed laws which would determine the future. For him, it was the individual in history that counted.

On the Zionist Left, Borochov tried to develop a socialist theory on the Jewish question since Marxism was decidedly weak in its consideration of Jews and the national question. Marx argued that the class struggle arose because of the clash between the forces of production and the existing relations of production. Borochov argued that under normal conditions of production, the class struggle would certainly take place, but under abnormal conditions the national struggle dominated. When a society was subjected to abnormal conditions of production such as the absence of territory, the class struggle could not fully be engaged in as long as the national question had not been settled. This, Borochov maintained, was the Jewish situation. He concluded that the Jewish working class was the promoter of the national ideal out of necessity and not out of nationalist conviction.

In his writings, Borochov demonstrated that the Jews had an abnormal economic structure. Technological advances would replace those in 'the lighter forms of production', with the result that Jewish labour would become displaced and the lower middle classes would become proletarianized. Only emigration to Palestine could normalize this situation. Socialist Zionism therefore required a strategic base 'to assure the normal conditions of production, but also to assure the proletariat of a normal base for its class struggle'.

The years 1917–19 offered a window of opportunity to Zionist leaders. The Ottoman Empire had been decisively defeated and had been dismantled as a consequence. New states such as Yugoslavia emerged in the Balkans. In the Middle East the British and the French set about dissecting the Arab world into a series of nation states to accommodate their imperial interests. The British had conquered Palestine and ruled it under General Allenby and the army.

Moreover, Zionist sympathisers such as David Lloyd-George now occupied the highest offices in government. Such an unprecedented development manifested itself in the promise of the Balfour Declaration, made in 1917 by Britain's Foreign Secretary, to establish a National Home in Palestine for the Jewish people while 'nothing should be done which may prejudice the civil and religious rights of existing non-Jewish communities in Palestine'. The deliberate vagueness and ambiguity of the Declaration – there was no mention of a Jewish state – allowed Balfour's successors to reinterpret its meaning in the changed circumstances of British interests after World War I. By the 1920s Zionist policy under Chaim Weizmann began to stagnate owing to repeated British attempts to row back from the original understanding of the Declaration. The first High Commissioner in Palestine, Sir Herbert Samuel, attempted in vain to balance the national aspirations of Arabs and Jews. Churchill's White Paper of 1922 challenged Weizmann's off-the-cuff comment and latent belief that Palestine would become as Jewish as England was English.

The impasse in advancing Zionist goals led to a split in the movement. Although all its succeeding leaders claimed to be following in Herzl's footsteps, Vladimir Jabotinsky argued that his dynamism had actually been replaced by a pedestrian diplomacy of inaction and acquiescence. Though an admirer of Britain, Jabotinsky was not reticent in openly criticizing British politicians and policy. Opposing the British decision to partition Palestine to create the new state of Jordan, he asserted that the Zionist aim should be clear and unambiguous – a Jewish state, sooner rather than later, on both banks of the Jordan. All this contrasted dramatically with the measured approach of Weizmann and the mainstream movement. In 1925 Jabotinsky established the Revisionist Zionist movement, which projected a robust approach to the question of a Jewish national home in Palestine:

> What has happened to the present Zionist generation is precisely what happened to the generation of Hebrews who left Egypt four thousand years ago. They had just enough spirit to rebel against their conditions and start on the big trail. Once on the trail, however, they carried most of the slave's moral toxins in their blood. One is the inveterate worship of the wealthy – *geverim* is the name. For centuries our forebears have been accustomed to entrust the *geverim* with all public business. The leaders of the present Zionist Executive, themselves little more than a refurbished and ornamented edition of this spirit, have most naturally exploited this inborn tendency in the Jew.[48]

Jabotinsky saw himself as the mentor of the 'new Jew' who would make a break with the pusillanimity and humiliation of the past: 'The ghetto despised physical manhood, the principle of male power as understood and worshipped by all free peoples in history. Physical courage and physical force was of no use, prowess of the body rather an object of ridicule. The only true heroism of the Ghetto acknowledged was that of self-suppression and dogged obedience to the Will above.'[49]

He was a brilliant orator and insightful writer – a fact recognized by his many opponents. His brand of self-sacrifice and romanticism appealed most powerfully to Jewish youth in interwar Eastern Europe. He told disadvantaged, discriminated against and impoverished young Jews in the Poland of the 1930s that they wore the crown of King David and they would build the Jewish state in their lifetime. Jabotinsky saw his mission as inspiring a new generation of Jews who would translate words into action. His youth movement, Betar, was modelled on the Sokol movement of Masaryk's Czechoslovakia. Yet their brown shirts – the colour of the soil of the Land of Israel – and their predilection for militancy led to accusations of fascism from their left-wing socialist opponents.

Jabotinsky grew up in Odessa, the cradle of Zionist activity. Recent discoveries in the Soviet archives have disclosed that he was not blessed with even the most rudimentary understanding of Judaism and Jewish life in general. Even the marginalized Herzl was better acquainted with Jewish affairs. Zionism came to Jabotinsky at an ideological, intellectual and psychological crossroads in his life – and he embraced the possibility of personal and national revival with passion:

> We were sitting at the time in the gutter, at the end of the great highway of life and on this road we watched the majestic procession of nations on their way to their historic destinies. And we were sitting aside, like beggars with outstretched hands, begging for alms and swearing in different languages that we merited the charitable offering. Sometimes it was given to us, and then it appeared that we were pleased and contented because the master was in a good mood and had thrown us a gnawed bone. So it only appeared, for deep in our souls was growing a repulsive disgust for the beggar's spot in the gutter and for the outstretched hand, and we felt a confused attraction for the great highway, a desire to walk upon it like others, not to beg but to build our own happiness.[50]

He depicted Herzl as his messiah. Before, he was lost; but now he was found:

We changed; we were brought to life by touching the earth upon which he moved. It is only recently that I felt that earth and it is only from that moment that I understood what it meant to live and breathe – and if on the morrow I should have awakened to learn that this was merely a dream, that I am what I had been, and that ground is not and cannot be under my feet, I would have killed myself, for it is impossible for one who has breathed the mountain air to return and be reconciled to sprawl once more in the gutter.[51]

Jabotinsky founded the Jewish Legion, which saw action in Palestine during World War I. In his famous article 'Afn Pripitshek' (By the Fireside)[52], he urged Jews to 'learn to shoot', for no one else would defend them. Through the Betar youth group he inspired downtrodden youth to be strong and proud. Yet Jabotinsky was in many ways a romantic nationalist, a nineteenth-century liberal conservative who looked to Garibaldi, Mazzini and Cavour, the heroes of the Italian Risorgimento. As the storm clouds gathered over Europe in the 1930s and Jewish nationalists began to respond to Arab attacks in Palestine, Jabotinsky found that control over his movement – and in particular Betar – was slipping from his hands. Despite his mesmerizing and combative rhetoric, he still believed in diplomacy and negotiation with England.

In 1923 he had advocated an 'Iron Wall' – an armed Jewish self-defence force to protect Jewish settlements against attacks by Arab nationalists. Jabotinsky argued that any force should be used for defensive and not offensive purposes. The 1930s were, however, a polarizing decade and Jabotinsky's youthful acolytes began to ask what was the purpose of military training and learning to shoot if not to use weapons in difficult times. Young nationalists in Palestine were inspired by far-Right intellectuals such as Abba Achimeir and Yehoshua Heschel Yeivin and the fiery nationalist poetry of Uri Zvi Greenberg. The emergence of the Irgun Zvai Leumi and its policy of retaliation against Arab attacks led Jabotinsky to make a failed attempt to exert control over their activities before death claimed him in 1940. In the last year of his life Betar effectively transferred its allegiance from the Revisionist movement to the Irgun.

This was carried out under the leadership of Menachem Begin, who pursued a policy of military Zionism often in opposition to Jabotinsky's wishes. As far back as 1932 Begin had supported the radical maximalist wing of the Revisionist movement, which advocated a more militant stand and a split from the mainstream Zionist Organization. As the situation deteriorated in both Europe and Palestine, the maximalists began to oppose the policy of *havlagah* – self-restraint in responding to Arab attacks – which was pursued by Weizmann, Ben-Gurion and the Zionist leaders. Begin and the maximalists were seen by the youth as responding to the needs of the moment. Maximalist Zionism gradually displaced Revisionist Zionism in the affections of Betar members. At a Betar conference in Warsaw in September 1938, Begin proclaimed the third stage of Zionism, 'military Zionism'. This, he argued, had superseded both practical Zionism and political Zionism. Jabotinsky vehemently disagreed, comparing Begin's ideas and rhetoric to the irritating creaking of a door. Yet Begin won the vote and the adherence of Betar. By early 1939 he had become the head of Betar in Poland, displacing less militant figures. The following year a sudden fatal heart attack removed Jabotinsky from the political struggle. The path to his reinvention and the selective exploitation of his ideas was now freely enacted by the maximalists.

Jabotinsky was initially admired by the Labour Zionists for his absorbing rhetoric and brilliant insights, but criticized for the futility of his political vision. Ultimately they believed that his vision would end in glorious failure. Weizmann's wife attempted to persuade Jabotinsky – with a distinct lack of success – to take on the role of inspirer and educator rather than dance on the minefield of politics. The Labour Zionists believed that they were creating a new kind of society, a Jewish workers' state, which would become the admired model for other developing nations. They also thought that the Zionist–Arab problem could be solved by appealing to the common goals of working people. The Revisionists were increasingly seen as impeding this dream. Jabotinsky's espousal of Max Nordau's *muskeljudentum* (muscular Judaism) as an ideological template was very far from their worship of the brotherhood of man. The Socialist Zionists preached integration rather than separatism. By the early 1930s the Zionist Left had come to abhor the Zionist Right with a deep and passionate hatred which often led to violent clashes. In an age of ideology the members of Betar in their brown uniforms were seen as home-grown fascists. In the eyes of the Labour movement Jabotinsky and his acolytes were the central obstacle to the realization of the dawn of socialism. After all, the Revisionists and Betar had condemned socialist economic enterprises, broken strikes, lauded nationalist triumphalism, revered religious tradition and raised individualism over the collective. The Right was seen as unpredictable and unstable, preferring the theatrical nature of politics, the boom and the bluster, to the concrete task of state building.

The second *aliyah*, the wave of immigration between 1903 and 1914, brought a cohort of Marxists, refugees from the failed 1905 Revolution in Russia. Among them were David Ben-Gurion and Yitzhak Ben-Zvi. The slogan of these immigrants was 'We have come to the Land to build her and to be built by her'. They believed in *halutziut* – the ardour of pioneering – and out of their utopian determination emerged the kibbutz and the *moshav* (collective settlement). Their Zionism was coloured by Marx and Tolstoy and by the Russian revolutionary tradition. The socialist Jewish state would be built by the workers who would mould the new society in their image. The Histadrut, founded in 1920, was a coalition of trade unions which was conceived primarily as the engine of state building. It became the entrepreneur of building in the physical sense. It embraced Solel Boneh, a building company; Koor, which owned factories; Hamashbir, the wholesale supplier for a chain of consumer cooperatives; and Kupat Holim, the workers' sick aid fund, which provided health care. It founded its own bank – Bank Ha'poalim, the Workers' Bank. Its economic and cooperative activities were based on the kibbutz. During the inter-war years Histadrut membership grew from 4000 to 100,000. Ben-Gurion, first as secretary-general of the Histadrut and then as chairman of the Jewish Agency from 1935, ensured that the Labour Zionists would be the leading political force in creating a Jewish workers' state, by creating facts on the ground in founding new kibbutzim and developing the Histadrut. The industrialization of Palestine in the 1930s meant that a quarter of all Jews belonged to the Histadrut. Its political reflection was Mapai, which not only led the Histadrut but also became the leading social-democratic party in the Zionist Congresses. It espoused a gradualist and pragmatic approach. To its left was Mapam, which believed in the Soviet Union and fervently hoped that it would turn away from its traditional anti-Zionist stand. It believed that any new society should be based on real socialism – the public ownership of land, the separation of state and religion and full equality for the Arab minority.

Ben-Gurion, however, had moved away from his original Marxist ideas. Borochov's theories, formulated in Russia, did not fit the reality of Palestine, where the class strata of European states hardly existed. The basic problem in the first decades of the twentieth century was one of sheer survival. The Zionists' ideal shifted from fighting the class war to building a society distinctly different from those they had left behind in Europe. Ben-Gurion reasoned that the working class had to take control and to move from 'a class to a nation'. This, he argued, could not be carried out without cooperating with non-socialists and indeed formally abandoning the class struggle.

The war years brought a tremendous growth in the number of factories and increased productivity to help the Allied war effort. In Palestine 136,000 Jews volunteered to enlist in the British forces. By contrast, the Palestinian national leadership sought refuge in Nazi Germany for the duration of the war. The cohesion of the Yishuv under the aegis of the Labour Zionists during this period provided a stable base from which to inflict defeat on the Arab armies in 1948. Yet the establishment of the state of Israel in May of that year effectively brought an end to the ethos of the pre-1948 state-in-waiting. Ben-Gurion's emphasis on statism and nationalism soon superseded socialist principle. Moreover, Labour Zionism had to become broader and amorphous to attract the many new immigrants who did not warm to socialism. By the 1950s the need for huge amounts of capital to stabilize the state and to absorb hundreds of thousands of new immigrants determined a capitalist future for Israel. Noah Lucas has written:

> The embryonic socialist society was supplanted by a capitalist order run by a labour bureaucracy. The popular conception of socialism was reduced to social-democratic welfarism within a capitalist society, while the more radical vision of workers' autarchy and social justice within a society controlled by the

Labour movement was relegated to the fringe of politics. To all intents and purposes, innovative socialism became a utopia, as though it were a promise about the future that would materialize when the state had time for it.[53]

Religion and the Question of Identity

The rise of Zionism posed the greatest challenge to the religious leadership of the Jews. Although many rabbis realized that there was growing criticism of their leadership in a time of change, there was also uncertainty about how to interpret the new situation. On one level the rise of Zionism challenged their authority and standing within communities. On another, it was believed that Zionism carried the seeds of secularization. There was much confusion. The man credited with coining the word 'Zionism' in 1885, Nathan Birnbaum, finished his days as a leading member of the anti-Zionist ultra-orthodox Agudat Yisrael party.

The ultra-orthodox were very clear in their denunciation of Zionism. Their lives were based on strict adherence to Jewish law. Every action of their lives was governed by the traditional interpretation of Judaism. They turned their backs on modern variants of Judaism such as the modern orthodox or the Reform movement. Interaction with the outside world was controlled and they were committed to separation from other bodies of thought and philosophy. As other Jews moved towards acculturation – and sometimes assimilation and conversion – they moved deeper into the Jewish world and therefore viewed Zionism as merely another by-product of the clash with modernity. They saw Herzl as no more than another false messiah – the latest in a long line of pretenders who had peppered Jewish history. Rabbinic authorities such as Moses Schreiber, known as the Hatam Sofer, simply rebuilt the spiritual walls of the ghetto after 1815 to repel the influence of both the *Haskalah* and the French Revolution. Schreiber was reputed to have commented that 'whatever is new is forbidden by the Torah'.

The very idea of a return to the historic homeland before the coming of the Messiah was seen as a forcing of God's hand. Human intervention in such things could not be justified. According to the Babylonian Talmud, Jews could not travel to the Land of Israel en masse. Neither should they rebel against the nations of the world.[54] There was little desire to disturb the docility of centuries, no matter how bad the situation. Zionism, like socialism, was viewed as a revolutionary movement which would lure Jews away from the path of righteousness. When Napoleon embarked on the invasion of Russia in 1812, many downtrodden Jews looked forward to a French victory to rid them of their reactionary oppressors. Not so Shneur Zalman of Lyady, the founder of the Lubavicher Hasidim, who feared that the legions of Napoleon would ultimately estrange the Jews from God. It was far better to remain under the despotic rule of the Tsar despite the poverty and oppression.

For those who came out of the world of ultra-orthodoxy and were learned, such as Ahad Ha'am, the rebuilding of the ghetto walls did not solve the crisis within Judaism. Ahad Ha'am argued that not only had the Jews come out of the ghetto but so too had Judaism. A plethora of Judaisms and Jewish identities had been spawned and this very fragmentation threatened the 'essential being' of the people. Ahad Ha'am made a distinction between the oppressed East and the emancipated West in the European Jewish experience:

The eastern form of the spiritual problem is absolutely different from the western. In the West it is the problem of the Jews; in the east, the problem of Judaism. The first weighs on the individual; the second on the nation. The one is felt by Jews who have had a European education; the other, by Jews whose education has been Jewish. The one is a product of antisemitism, and is dependant on antisemitism for its existence; the other is a natural product of a real link with a millennial culture, and it will remain unsolved and unaffected even if the troubled of the Jews are all over the world, attain comfortable economic positions, are on the best possible terms with their neighbours, and are admitted to the fullest social and political equality.[55]

In his essay 'The Negation of the Diaspora' (1909) Ahad Ha'am postulated that those Jews who had entered the mainstream of European life could not survive as a scattered people. Orthodoxy no longer provided a bulwark against 'the ocean of foreign culture which threatens to obliterate our national characteristics and traditions and thus gradually to put an end to our existence as a people'.[56] The threat of eventual extinction led Jews along two paths. One group eagerly embraced assimilation as a means of ditching Judaism and Jewishness, while the other was unable or unwilling to assimilate. The latter contemplated that it had to 'put an end to our dispersion before it puts an end to us'. Both stances were valid solutions to the problem of Judaism, Ahad Ha'am argued, and said that different types of Jews would take different paths.

His appeal was addressed essentially to those rationalist Jews who noted the changing nature of Judaism. Yet there were other Jews who remained true to the traditions of their fathers but desired a synthesis of Judaism and the proposed return to Zion. They believed that the anti-Zionist ultra-orthodox were rigidly conservative in their approach while Ahad Ha'am and his followers were too radical and quasi-secular in theirs. Two rabbis, Yehuda Chai Alkalai and Zvi Hirsh Kalischer, were highly influenced by the times and societies in which they lived. The effects of the French Revolution in particular caused them to reinterpret the oaths in the Babylonian Talmud. What did 'en masse' mean? One, one hundred, one thousand? If Jews went in small numbers to the Holy Land, as did the followers of the great sage the Vilna Gaon a hundred years previously, surely this was not 'en masse'. What about the return of the Jews from exile in Babylon, guided by the prophets Nechemiah and Ezra, in order to build the Second Temple – was this 'en masse'?

These religious proto-Zionists placed great emphasis on reclaiming the land. In 1836 Kalischer approached the banker Amschel Mayer Rothschild to purchase territory in Palestine. Kalischer, who was the rabbi of Thorn in Prussia, also wrote to Sir Moses Montefiore, a leader of Anglo-Jewry, urging him to establish settlements in Palestine. In 1867 he made 'An Appeal to Our Brethren' to support 'the colonization, cultivation and improvement' of the 'abandoned, devastated, sacred soil'.[57]

Other religious scholars, such as the Italian philosopher and translator Samuel David Luzzatto, had similar ideas. He wrote in 1854 that 'Palestine must be peopled by Jews and tilled by them in order that it flourish economically and agriculturally and take on beauty and glory'.[58] There is no doubt that the nineteenth-century national liberation movements which struggled against great empires for their independence made a profound impression. Shortly after the unification of Italy, Rabbi Kalischer published *Drishat Zion* (Seeking Zion). He asked:

Why do the people of Italy and of other countries sacrifice their lives for the land of their fathers, while we, like men bereft of strength and courage, do nothing? Are we inferior to all other peoples, who have no regard for life and fortune as compared with the love of their land and nation? Let us take to heart the examples of the Italians, Poles and Hungarians, who laid down their lives and possessions in the struggle for national independence, while we, the children of Israel, who have the most glorious and holiest of lands as our inheritance, are spiritless and silent.[59]

Max Nordau, Herzl's close colleague, who had long ago distanced himself from his religious background, pointed out in 1902 that the new Zionism was neither mystical nor messianic. Herzl also remained loyal to his secular liberal principles and was aware of the strong opposition of Eastern European Zionists to rabbinical intervention. He vowed to prevent any 'theocratic tendencies' from coming to the fore in the future Jewish state. He promised, in *The Jewish State*, to keep 'the priests within the confines of their temples' in the same fashion as 'we shall keep our professional army within the confines of their barracks'. Yet, unlike Nordau, Weizmann and Ahad Ha'am, Herzl's sparse Jewish background produced a lack of both discernment and prejudice towards the rabbis. Weizmann later wrote:

Herzl had excessive respect for the Jewish clergy, born not of intimacy, but of distance. He saw something rather occult and mysterious in the rabbis, while he knew them as individuals, good, bad or indifferent. His leaning towards clericalism distressed us, so did this touch of Byzantinism in his manner. Almost from the outset, a kind of court sprang up about him, of worshippers who pretended to guard him from too close contact with the mob. I am compelled to say certain elements in his bearing invited such an attitude.[60]

While Weizmann wanted to break with the past and the influence of the rabbis, Herzl had to take note of rabbinical authority and power if he wished to 'conquer the Jewish community'. Herzl also had to contend with the declarations of the *Protestrabbiner* – mainly German Reform rabbis who collectively condemned Zionism on the eve of the first Zionist Congress in 1897. Significantly they supported 'the noble efforts directed towards the colonization of Palestine by Jewish agriculturists', but vehemently opposed its translation into the building blocks of an embryonic Jewish state. It was not only their religious calling which impelled them to condemn Zionism but also a sense of loyalty to their host countries. If the nineteenth century had borne witness to the struggle of Jews to win the same rights as any other citizen of the country, then Zionism threatened to upset the ongoing campaign to maintain these gains as well as to impede the securing of them in less enlightened lands. On the eve of the first Zionist Congress American rabbis declared: 'Such attempts do not benefit, but infinitely harm our Jewish brethren where they are still persecuted, by confirming the assertion of their enemies that the Jew are foreigners in the countries in which they are at home, and of which they are everywhere the most loyal and patriotic citizens.'[61]

The feared accusation of double loyalties struck deeply at those Jews who wished to acculturate. This was particularly the case in Germany, where Jews flocked to the nationalist standard. It was only the rise of Nazism that brutally confronted the most assimilated of German Jews with the most tortuous of dilemmas. Thus while the Zionist Albert Einstein refused to return to Germany, the assimilated Fritz Haber – whose chemical genius saved Germany from early defeat in World War I through the Haber Process, in which ammonia is manufactured synthetically – was forced to leave. On Hitler's accession to power there were even minuscule groups of Jews such as Hans Joachim Schoeps's Deutsche Vortrupp and Max Neumann's Verband nationaldeutscher Juden which proclaimed their loyalty to the Führer and the Fatherland.[62] Even the destruction of European Jewry did not always produce a resolution of such intrinsic questions of identity. Some Holocaust survivors returned to Germany while others emigrated to Israel.

This contrasted with a great Jewish pride in Germany some forty years previously, when there was not so much resentment against Zionism as incomprehension. The literary historian Ludwig Geiger wrote in 1905 that Zionism was incompatible with the German spirit:

> The German Jew who has a voice in German literature must, as he has been accustomed to for the last century and a half, look upon Germany alone as his fatherland, upon the German language as his mother tongue, and the future of the German nation must remain the only one upon which he bases his hopes. Any desire to form together with his coreligionists a people outside of Germany is, not to speak of its impracticability, downright thanklessness towards the nation in whose midst he lives – a chimera; for the German Jew is a German in his national peculiarities, and Zion is for him the land only of the past, not of the future.[63]

Geiger was the son of Abraham Geiger, one of the founders of Reform Judaism in Europe. It was not only the ultra-orthodox who condemned Zionism but also their opponents in the Reform and Liberal movements. In 1885 the Pittsburgh platform, adopted by the Central Conference of American (Reform) Rabbis, utterly rejected the idea of a Jewish nation.

Indeed it was Reform opponents of Zionism who ensured a change of venue, from Munich to Basel, for the first Zionist Congress in 1897. For both the ultra-orthodox and the Reform, the Holocaust proved to be a potent leveller of previously held views.

Despite Herzl's diplomacy in attempting to prevent factionalism within the new movement, schisms occurred within a few years. In 1901 the decision was taken to introduce 'cultural activities' into the Zionist movement. The meaning of 'Zionist education' was interpreted differently by Religious Zionists and the disciples of Ahad Ha'am. Weizmann argued that cultural activities had to be based on the history of the people and not the history of Judaism. Religious Zionists, in response, argued that it was absurd to eliminate God from any teaching of Zionism. Weizmann formed his Democratic Faction in 1901 while Rabbi Yitzhak Reines established the Mizrachi movement in Vilna in 1902. In their manifesto the adherents of Mizrachi declared: 'We have always been united by that ancient hope, by the promise which lies at the very roots of our religion, namely that only out of Zion will the Lord bring redemption to the people of Israel. The emancipation which our German brethren so desired did much to divide us and keep us scattered in the countries of our dispersion. When the limbs are dispersed, the body disintegrates, and when there is no body, the spirit has no place in this world.'[64]

Try as it might, the Mizrachi movement could not shift successive Zionist Congresses from their understanding of 'cultural activities'. A split occurred within Mizrachi between those who wished to leave the formal Zionist movement and those who wanted to remain. The minority who left joined with the ultra-orthodox in 1912 to form the mainstay of the religious anti-Zionist Agudat Yisrael party.

4

What is Zionism Today?

The Origins of Anguish

Why, then, has progressive humankind turned its back on Zionism? An obvious explanation is the changing nature of the state of Israel, the rise of Palestinian nationalism and the Israeli occupation of the West Bank and Gaza since 1967. But there are deeper reasons which go beyond the Israel–Palestine conflict. These are rooted in how the European Left has viewed the Jews and their national movements since the downfall of Napoleon. Arthur Hertzberg commented that 'the leaders of Western opinion do not know how to deal with Jews when they are not victims'.[65] The continued existence and survival of the Jews was never adequately explained by the Left. The Jews were somehow always out of ideological focus and this blurring extended to Zionism. Since Zionism was different and difficult to categorize, some argued that logically it must be wrong. Moreover, the Left accused Zionists of diverting Jewish attention away from the class struggle – a nationalist distraction from the task of building international socialism. Lenin refused to accept any kind of Jewish national movement, regardless of whether it was the Marxist Zionism of Borochov or the anti-Zionism of the Bund. Such differences were suspended during the common struggle of the Jews and the Left against fascism. The shock of the Holocaust forged an even deeper alliance. Succeeding generations of the Left inherited these sentiments, but neither the experiences nor the background.

While there was definitely a love affair between the Jews and the Left which reached its apogee in the fight against fascism, there has been an increasing antagonism between them since 1967. There has been a continuing disappointment among Jews on the Left that Jews are often abandoned in their hour of need. It happened in 1881 in Russia when the revolutionary movement *Narodnaya Volia* espoused the cause of the pogromists. It happened in May 1967 when members of the New Left were silent when Israel was threatened by surrounding Arab states – and this was before the establishment of settlements on the West Bank and Gaza. Today Diaspora opponents of the policies of successive Israeli governments feel betrayed by the European Left's lack of support for the Israeli peace camp. Instead there is a groundswell of support for campaigns such as the boycott of Israeli academics, many of whom are fully paid-up members and even founders of the peace movement. Instead of attacking government policies, such activities actually victimize their most vociferous opponents.

Yosef Gorny has explained that the utopian vision of the New Left in 1967 was one-dimensional whereas the Jewish national Left was three-dimensional in that in addition to establishing a new society it wished to revive Jewish national culture and 'transform Israel into the ideal Jewish society'.[66] But is this parlous state of affairs between the Jews and the Left merely a blip in their long relationship? Or is it something far more fundamental? In fact, has there always been an ideological difference between the Jewish national Left and the European Left?

The French Revolution was welcomed as a complete break with the past by European Jews. In Colmar, for example, the entire Jewish community was burned at the stake in 1349. Those who resettled there were once more expelled in 1512. Even visiting Jewish merchants were forbidden to trade there. The French Revolution made amends. It rescinded the tax levied by the good burghers of Colmar on Jews and cattle that passed through its gates. But the exponents of the Revolution defined the basis on which Jews should be seen by the wider public. Comte Stanislaus de Clermont-Tonnerre remarked in the National Assembly in 1789: 'Everything must be refused to the Jews as a nation; everything must be granted to them as individuals. They must be citizens. It is claimed that they do not wish to be citizens. Let them say so and let them be banished; there cannot be a nation within a nation.'[67]

This continued into the radical phase of the Revolution, when Robespierre and the Jacobins ruled France. The new France was to be a single nation and the emancipation of the Jews a profoundly symbolic act of breaking with the past. The act of emancipation, no matter how welcomed by the Jews and how heartfelt by the revolutionaries, did not reflect the reality in which the Jews found themselves. The proposed emancipation certainly met the demands of Enlightenment theory, but it left the Jews in a quandary. In a speech on the eve of the Revolution, the Comte de Mirabeau placed the offer before them: 'Gentlemen! Are our laws your laws? Are our courts of justice yours too? Are you legally our fellow citizens, our brethren? Will you be able to take the civic oath in your hearts as well as by word of mouth? If such be the case, excellent! Then you are good Frenchmen, then you will be active citizens.

If not, then remain passive citizens and wait until your city, Jerusalem is rebuilt and there you can be active or passive as you choose.'[68]

Of course, most Jews were eager to enter through the portals of emancipation into French society and to leave the detested ghetto behind, but at what price? It was easy to rebuild the ghetto walls and pretend that the Revolution had simply passed by. At the other extreme, it was just as easy to convert. The hardest part of the bargain with modernity was to be in the middle, to be both a Jew and a contributing member of society. But what was unknown was the extent to which a society demanded the expunging of Jewish characteristics. After all, Benjamin Disraeli, who was a baptized Jew, often identified with Jewish concerns and became a great British Prime Minister as a one-nation Tory. In contrast, Adolphe Isaac Crémieux, who did not convert, became Minister of Justice in numerous French governments and a stalwart of Jewish communal endeavours. Were Disraeli and Crémieux exceptions to the rule or symbolic steps on the road to true emancipation? Such questions assumed less importance after 1848, when nationalism became the prerogative of the nationalists and modern anti-Semitism raised its head in a systematic, authorized fashion.

Many Jews took advantage of the opportunities thrown up by the French Revolution and rushed to cover all discernible traces of their Jewishness. With the return of the forces of reaction – especially in the Rhineland – many Jews divested themselves of their Jewishness through conversion and assimilation in order not to lose their hard-won privileges. Löb Baruch thus became Ludwig Börne. Others, such as the poet Heinrich Heine, nominally converted while privately confiding that they never truly left the faith. Common to all these Jews was a state of psychological torment as to who they really were and where they really belonged. Some poured out their frustration on the Jews from whom they were attempting to free themselves. Victor Adler, the father of Austrian socialism, was always troubled by his Jewish background. When asked about anti-Semitism he commented: 'My dear comrade, one must have Jews, only not too many.' Similarly, Rosa Luxemburg attempted to transcend anti-Semitism by regarding it as a pernicious aspect of bourgeois society. She commented: 'For the followers of Marx, as for the working class, the Jewish question as such does not exist, just as the "Negro question" or the "Yellow Peril" does not exist. From the standpoint of the working class, the Jewish question . . . is a question of racial hatred as a symptom of social reaction, which, to a certain extent, is an indivisible part of all societies based on class antagonism.'[69]

Many German-Jewish intellectuals in particular, emerging from such a convoluted, confusing background, entered the early socialist movement, often as its theorists. Through the universalism of socialism they could escape the particularism of Judaism. Ferdinand Lassalle, the founder of the forerunner of the German Social Democratic Party, was a traditional non-Jewish Jew who also attempted to purge himself of past affiliations: 'I do not like the Jews at all; indeed in general I abhor them. I see in them only degenerate sons of a great, but long past age. In the course of centuries of bondage those people acquired the characteristics of slaves, and this is why I am extremely unfavourable to them.'[70]

By the end of the nineteenth century Jews who wished to change their own Jewishness had a plethora of choices, of which Communism and Zionism were but two options. Quite often accidental factors pushed the actors in one direction rather than another. Jabotinsky and Trotsky came from similar backgrounds, studied in Odessa and were oblivious to their Jewishness. Given their early histories, it is not far-fetched to postulate that Jabotinsky could have espoused Communism and Trotsky Jewish nationalism. Max Nordau, the son of a rabbi, changed his name from Simon Südfeld (southern field) to Max Nordau (northern meadow) in an attempt to escape his Jewishness. Yet he became one of the founders of the modern Zionist movement. In an address to the first Zionist Congress in 1897, he thanked Rousseau and the Encyclopaedists for the fruits of the French Revolution, but argued that the emancipation of the Jews did not come out of any fraternal feeling for the Jews – 'the men of 1792 emancipated us only for the sake of logic'. The liberation of the Jews was merely an automatic application of rationalism. The Jews, he stated, were allowed to believe for one or two generations that they belonged to other national groups, but the anti-Semitism of the late nineteenth century indicated that this had been a delusion of grand proportions:

> The emancipated Jew is insecure in his relations with his fellow man, timid with strangers, and suspicious even of the secret feelings of his friends. His best powers are dissipated in suppressing and destroying, or at least in the difficult task of concealing his true character. He fears that this character might be recognized as Jewish, and he never has the satisfaction of revealing himself as he is in his real identity, in every thought and sentiment, in every physical gesture. He has become a cripple within, and a counterfeit person without, so that like everything unreal, he is ridiculous and hateful to all men of high standards.[71]

Some sections of the Left – especially those Jews who were shedding their Jewishness – reacted strongly to such assertions. The Bolsheviks in particular relied on the advice of their Jewish members, the *Yevsektsia*, in opposing all forms of Jewish nation-alism. After the October Revolution Zionism was gradually suppressed resulting in mass arrests and deportation in September 1924. Some members of Zionist groups visited the Gulag four or five times between the 1920s and 1968, when the Soviet Union first permitted a trickle of Jews to emigrate to Israel. Hebrew was also suppressed in 1919 despite eloquent appeals from Jewish educators:

> [Anatoly] Lunacharsky [First Soviet Commissar for Education and the Arts] sat there all the time, leaning on his elbows, his head resting on his hands, listening . . . when we had finished our speeches (in support of Hebrew) he got up and moved away, along the wall, leaving it to his deputy to answer. It was at this moment that we understood what Lunacharsky had meant on the eve of the meeting when he had said: 'I am the only one to protect you.' We saw that there had not been any need for the Yevsektsia [Jewish Communists] to be represented; they had meanwhile worked on Pokrovsky in their own way, and the latter, not unwillingly, had taken on their task. We again lis-tened to the routine phrases of the bourgeoisie that was hoodwinking the proletariat with its ideology of the 'dead' Hebrew language, which was nothing but the heritage of cleri-calism and so on and so forth . . .'[72]

The barbarity of the Russian civil war persuaded many Jewish nationalists to side with the 'Reds' rather than the anti-Semitic 'Whites'. Communism was clearly no flash in the pan. They joined a disproportionate number of assimilated Jews in the upper echelons of the Communist Party such as Trotsky, Zinoviev, Kamenev, Sverdlov and Radek. In reality Soviet rule meant a gradual stripping away of all vestiges of Jewish life. Yet in the 1920s Jewish Communists attempted to construct an alternative to the traditionalist religious past and to nationalist rival ideologies such as Bundism and Zionism. The Jewish New Year was replaced by celebration of the October Revolution. The traditional *challot* (plaited Sabbath bread) mutated into the shape of a hammer and sickle. Baby boys were named Melik (Marx–Engels–Lenin–International Communism) and girls Ninel (Lenin backwards). A Jewish autonomous republic, Birobidzhan, came into existence on the border with China. All these innovations died with their initiators in the Stalinist purges. Jewishness was never a positive attribute in the USSR, but its disappearance was. Indeed the Soviet authorities went to great lengths to suppress the fact that Lenin's maternal great-grandfather was the Jew Moshko Blank.[73] Russian anti-Semitism periodically bubbled up from the depths, especially during the last years of Stalin's life. Zionists and Jews were often indistinguishable in the Soviet press.

Communism originally seemed to embellish biblical prophecy and Jewish national aspirations to build a new society. It possessed a wide base of support because it offered to break the chains of the Jews as an ethnic group of oppressed workers. Jews flocked into the Communist Party in every European country. When the International Brigades were formed to confront fascism during the Spanish Civil War, of the fifty-four nationalities who fought, the Jews were disproportionately represented. Comparing the numbers of brigaders as a percentage of the population of their national group, Jews headed the list. Indeed Jews in Europe looked to the Soviet Union as the only force to stand up to fascism. Yet their illusions were totally dispelled when the Molotov–Ribbentrop pact was signed on the eve of World War II and Moscow subsequently handed over German-Jewish Communists to the Nazis.

Trotsky was asked in 1903 by the Bundist Vladimir Medem whether he considered himself a Russian or a Jew. He replied, 'I am a social democrat – and only that.' Yet later in life, in Mexican exile, he began to take an interest in the settlement experiment in Palestine – seemingly as a Jew – in a long private conversation with the socialist Zionist Beba Idelson in 1937.[74]

In 1947 Andrei Gromyko, the Soviet representative at the United Nations, made essentially Zionist speeches in support of a Jewish state – even though at the same time the NKVD, the forerunner of the KGB, was imprisoning young Jews who requested permission to emigrate to Palestine.

The European Left and the Christian Right

In Britain, Bertrand Russell overcame his reservations about a Jewish national home in Palestine. In 1943 he wrote: 'I have come gradually to see that, in a dangerous and largely hostile world, it is essential to Jews to have some country which is theirs, some region where they are not suspected aliens, some state which embodies what is distinctive in their culture.'[75]

The bitterness of the struggle against fascism and the revelations of the death and extermination camps after the war persuaded many on the Left that the Jews should be permitted to establish a liberal and enlightened state on the territory that they had purchased and built upon in Palestine. The Left pressed for an act of affirmative action on behalf of the Jews just as they did later for blacks and women. Indeed it was said that in the British Labour Party after the war, the further Left that you went, the more you were committed to Zionism. Aneurin Bevan was described 'as almost a Zionist'[76] and considered resigning from the Atlee government over British policy in

Palestine.[77] Anthony Wedgwood Benn, later Tony Benn, was a died-in-the-wool advocate for Israel and a regular contributor to the Labour Zionist *Jewish Vanguard*.

By the 1960s and especially after the Six Day War in 1967, opinion began to change – and it was not solely due to Israel's occupation of the West Bank and Gaza. Some older intellectuals such as Jean-Paul Sartre, Herbert Marcuse and I. F. Stone supported the old Israel. A new generation of the Left, however, struggled to secure a political identity after the revelation of Stalin's crimes. Many reclaimed Trotsky, Rosa Luxemburg and Antonio Gramsci as guides and icons. Such identification was located in a solidarity with Third World liberation movements. The neo-Maoist strategy of Yasser Arafat's Al Fatah after 1965 suggested that the Palestinian cause was an integral part of this broad struggle against colonialism and imperialism.

It therefore became easy for the emerging New Left to depict Zionism as merely another form of European colonialism. Zionism, a minority concern for Jews, was a hybrid of both nineteenth-century European and twentieth-century developing-world nation building. In Europe old nations such as France transformed themselves into nation states as the framework of definition.In the Third World indigenous elites in countries such as Ghana and Indonesia ousted the colonial power and proceeded to build a new nation out of the imposed colonial structure. Zionism was different. It had to reconstruct the Jewish nation in a period of ethnic consciousness, return it to the geographical cradle of its history, Palestine, remove the colonial power, Britain, and then proceed to build a new Israeli nation.[78] In an era of decolonization such complexity was pushed aside in favour of simpler explanations which better fitted conventional theory.

Yet the New Left did not emerge from the working class or

the ranks of the deprived. A great number of its adherents were middle class and in many cases students. In one sense a profound identification with liberation movements in often remote locations helped to create the distance from their own origins. Their parents may have viewed the Jews as a persecuted people with whom they expressed solidarity, but for the post-war generation, confronting fascism and anti-Semitism was incidental, not central. It was not a life-determining watershed. In 1959 Richard Crossman, the Oxford academic and Labour Minister, reflected:

> Was it that we were all on the lookout in 1939 for appeasement and saw the Arabs as a fascist force to which Jewish liberty was being sacrificed? Partly perhaps. But I suspect that six years of this war have fundamentally changed our emotions. We were pro-Jew emotionally in 1939 as part of 'anti-fascism'. We were not looking at the actual problems of Palestine, but instinctively standing up for Jews, whenever there was a chance to do so. Now, most of us are not emotionally pro-Jew, but only rationally 'anti-antisemitic' which is a very different thing.[79]

Opposing anti-Semitism did not mean philo-Semitism. It was the ideological inheritance from the French Revolution, when the Jews were almost incidental, that mattered. Support for Zionism was seen as a consequence of the struggle against fascism and not in terms of the struggle of the two national movements – Zionist Jewish and Palestinian Arab – that had existed before the rise of fascism. For the succeeding generation, which had neither the knowledge of the times nor the experience of living through them, the Zionist experiment was peripheral to their concerns. In one sense the New Left was never burdened by the problems of Crossman's generation. The rise of Palestinian nationalism after 1967 fitted much more readily into their world view. It became a case of 'Zionist villains and Palestinian heroes'.[80] In 1971 the editor of the *Guardian* refused to publish a private critical advertisement styled as 'an open letter to the Jews of Israel and the western World'.[81] In 1996 another *Guardian* editor published a half-page advertisement by Ayatollah Khomeini of Iran on the occasion of the Haj which implied 'Zionist' control of the US media.[82] McCarthyite definitions of Zionism seeped into the language of the Left. This, in part, owed its lineage to Soviet attempts to use 'Zionism' as a catch-all for all the evils in the world. Tom Paulin, the poet and writer, therefore defined the Blair government as 'a Zionist government'.[83]

More generally, Zionism was considered by the Left as an anomaly and Israel a mere accident of history. Yet at the radical edge of reason, Zionism was cast in a fantasy world of satanic forces. As Anthony Julius has remarked:

> The primary distinction is between the rational enemy and the irrational enemy. The rational enemy conceives his enmity in consequence of a real conflict with his adversary. He wishes either to promote an interest or a value that is contested by another party, or to defend one that is under threat by that party. That party thereby becomes his enemy. The enmity of the irrational enemy, by contrast, is conceived in fantasy. In consequence of entirely imaginary injuries or threats, he afflicts strangers.[84]

For the Left, such caricaturing of Zionism and confusion about Jewish nationalism per se marked in part a return to nineteenth-century theory about the Jews – emancipation for 'the sake of logic'. But for the post-war generation of Jews in the

Diaspora, the Holocaust was not a mere backdrop but recent if not living history in which they were touched by events. Many Jews of liberal views who opposed the occupation of the West Bank and supported a two-state solution were disturbed by this turn of events. Most could well distinguish between unpalatable news and biased news, but this was clearly something more fundamental. After 1967 the ideological differences between the Jewish national Left and the European Left over the meaning of Zionism became central.

Another factor which distanced the Left from Israel was the increasing support Israel gained from the Christian Right in the United States. Christian Zionists, who believe that the return of the Jews to the Holy Land would herald the second coming of Jesus Christ, had played a significant part in the Zionist saga. David Lloyd-George, who as Prime Minister engineered the passage of the Balfour Declaration in 1917, declared a few years later in a protest against anti-Semitism: 'If the Jew lives in a strange land, he must be persecuted and pogrommed out of it. If he wants to go back to his own land, he must be prevented. Through the centuries, in every land, whatever he does or intends to do, he has been pursued by the echo of the brutal cry of the rabble of Jerusalem against the greatest of Jews – "crucify him".'[85]

The Left believed that the alignment of George W. Bush's Republican administration with Ariel Sharon's policies was symptomatic of the former's Evangelical sympathies and his adherence to the Christian Right. Even so, both Jimmy Carter and Bill Clinton were also Christians who identified with the Zionist experiment yet attempted to bring Israelis and Palestinians together. The Clintons had gone to the Holy Land with their church, the Immanuel Baptist Church, as early as December 1981.[86] The Christian Right, however, practised none of the liberalism of these Democratic presidents and became increasingly identified with right-wing Republicanism. Moreover, there was an unspoken rift between American Jews who followed a liberal agenda and the Christian Right, which wished to eliminate any vestiges of liberalism from the body politic. Regardless of their socio-economic position, more than 70% of American Jews always voted for the Democrats – a percentage exceeded only by American blacks. The Christian Right also projected an agenda of conversion – both overt and covert – and began to resent the fact that American Jews stubbornly did not wish to see the religious light.

The Christian Right were not normative Christian Zionists. They did not wholly regard the Church as 'the new Israel'. It had neither superseded the Jews nor displaced Judaism. Since the Hebrew Bible spoke only of Jews and not their Christian inheritors, they argued that God must work in parallel – through both the old Israel and the new Church. Such Christian Dispensationalism had evolved in nineteenth-century America. The return of the Jews to their land became a prerequisite for the unfurling of future dispensations – epochs of time. There would be the epoch when true Christian believers would ascend to heaven. In another period a fraction of Jews would be saved after the raging destruction at Armageddon through the intervention of Jesus, who would then be recognized as the true saviour of Israel and acclaimed as its messiah. Although there are many variations on this theme,[87] the establishment of the state in 1948 and the capture of Jerusalem in 1967 were the real catalysts for the impassioned Zionist certainty of the Christian Right that emerged in the 1970s. Such events were evidence for the Dispensationalists that the previous Christian understanding of the role of Jews and Judaism had been erroneous.

The rise of the Christian Right in the US paralleled the rise of the Israeli Right. The election of Menachem Begin in 1977 marked the beginning of a remarkable partnership between the conservative Likud Party and the US evangelicals. The latter saw the borders of the Land of Israel in biblical terms. Genesis 15:18 states: 'To your seed I give this land from the river of Egypt to the great river, the river Euphrates.' Such a definition today would encompass parts of Egypt, Lebanon and even parts of Iraq. Yet the early Zionists did not base their proposed borders on those in the Bible. The contours of the first Zionist map in November 1918 were based on economic factors, access to water, efficient transportation facilities and the topography of the area. The Israeli Right, however, derived its ideological approach in part through opposition to the first partition of Palestine in the early 1920s, when the British hived off the East Bank of the Jordan to establish the state of Jordan. America's Christian Right and the Israeli Right shared the belief that the borders of Israel should extend as far as possible. Begin's governments cemented an alliance with the increasingly influential Christian Right and relied on figures such as Jerry Falwell and the Moral Majority during the Reagan era.

The Christian Right tended in general to oppose any moves that could lead to a rapprochement with both the Palestinians and the Arab world in general. For example, the International Christian Embassy, an evangelical institution based in Jerusalem, strongly condemned Menachem Begin when he agreed to return Sinai to the Egyptians. 'The Bible does not say you will receive half the land of Canaan. We are better Zionists than you Israelis. You don't fully believe in your cause.'[88] The Israeli Prime Minister Bibi Netanyahu was similarly criticized for the Hebron Agreement in 1997.[89] Any notion of 'land for peace' was condemned, as was a Palestinian state between Israel and Jordan. At a mass meeting of the National Unity Coalition in January 1998, Netanyahu addressed the evangelicals during the heat of the Lewinsky affair despite the entreaties of US Jewish organization not to deliberately antagonize the Clinton White House. The evangelical audience chanted in unison, 'Not one inch.' In contrast, a few years previously, Yossi Beilin, then deputy Foreign Minister and one of the architects of the Oslo Accords, blocked an official invitation to Ralph Reed, a director of the Christian Coalition, to visit Israel.

Yet both Israel's Labour and Likud parties courted the Christian Zionists because of their unequivocal support for Israel and their influence with Republican administrations. American Jewish organizations tended to be muted in their criticism of the Christian Right whenever either the Republicans or Likud were in power. Thus in 1994 when both Rabin and Clinton were in office, the Anti-Defamation League published a 200-page report entitled 'The Religious Right: The Assault on Tolerance and Pluralism in America'. Moreover, although Likud still worked with Christian organizations that projected an openly conversionist agenda, many mainstream Jewish organizations withdrew any form of cooperation. During the current Intifada, US Jewish organizations have had to drop their inhibitions and work with the Christian Right, not so much to prevent criticism of Sharon's policies as to inhibit the gradual delegitimization of Israel. In the context of the Islamization of the Israel–Palestine conflict, the Organization of the Islamic Conference Member States can muster fifty-seven votes in the United Nations. This number is increased by other members from the developing world. Such block votes mean that often there can be no rational debate on substantive issues. Israel, regardless of the legitimacy of any criticism, has to rely on the Bush administration's veto. Moreover, the Christian Right has been fortified by the arguments of the neo-conservatives in the Republican Party – many of whom emerged from the Left in the 1960s and subsequently warmed to the pronouncements of Likud.

Beyond the religious dimension, the US political Right also identifies with Zionism because it sees a shared history in the rejection by both of 'the old Europe'. The Israeli Right – whether the liberal-conservative Vladimir Jabotinsky or the maximalist Menachem Begin – looks back to both the American and French Revolutions as exemplars for the development of Zionism. Many Republicans view Zionism as an attempt to build a new society on values different from those of the societies that they had left. The Israeli Left, however, looked towards the radical Jacobin phase of the French Revolution. Indeed Ben-Gurion appreciated the Bolsheviks' single-mindedness. In 1923 he lauded Lenin as an example for Zionists. He characterized Lenin as tenacious and iron-willed – someone who was willing to sacrifice grown men and babes in arms to secure his goal, a radical of radicals 'who knows how to crawl on his stomach through deepest mire to gain his end'. The example of Lenin's ruthless expediency was admired not only by Ben-Gurion and Yitzhak Tabenkin on the Left, but also by Uri Zvi Greenberg and Abba Achimeir on the far Right. Yet Ben-Gurion differentiated himself from the romanticism on the Zionist Right. He committed to his diary in December 1923 the observation that Lenin was a figure 'who does not permit webs of phrases to entrap his thought and refuses to be entangled either by formula or doctrine. For this sharp and clear vision sees only naked reality, the brutal truth and the actual balance of forces.'[90]

Such an endorsement persuaded in 1948 many on the US Right, together with their allies in the conservative Arab states, that Israel would eventually become part of the Communist bloc allied with the USSR. Although such fears indicated a profound misunderstanding of the vehemence that Stalin's regime exhibited towards both Jews and Zionism, Pat Robertson, the founder of the Christian Coalition, carried on this tradition in his writings. Thus, although he praised Zionism and condemned any exchange of land for peace, he also alluded to a fissile admixture of Jewish communists and Jewish capitalists wielding considerable international influence. For Robertson, 'Communism was the brainchild of German-Jewish intellectuals', with Moses Hess cast in the pivotal role as 'the Communist rabbi'. He also refers to Nesta Webster's publication *Secret Societies and Subversive Movements*, which was required reading for British fascists both before and after World War II.[91] Attention has been drawn to the fact that Robertson has also referred to the works of George Sylvester Viereck, who was indicted as a German agent during World War II and sentenced to four years' imprisonment.[92]

5

Where to Next?

Between Right and Right

The tragedy of Zionism is that it arose at the same point in history as Arab nationalism. The Arab writer Najib Azouri commented in 1905 that the two movements were destined to fight each other until one of them prevailed. Azouri's observation was ominously prescient. Pan-Arabists considered Palestine an integral part of the *Umma*, the community of Muslims. The very idea of a Jewish entity in Palestine was seen as an impediment to this vision. Some Muslims found it difficult to conceive of the Jews occupying anything other than *dhimmi* status: protected but looked down upon by the host society. Many Christians, such as Azouri himself, were influenced by both Christian anti-Judaism and the new anti-Semitism of *fin de siècle* France. The policy of Turkification after the Young Turks' revolution of 1908, which sought to erode Arab identity through discriminatory policies, helped instead to define Arab identity and enhance Arab nationalism. Although there were discussions aimed at achieving an accommodation between Arabs and Jews on the eve of World War I, the fault lines were already clear.

The flowering of Arab nationalism after 1918 and the ascendancy of the Arab nation state coincided with the highpoint of Zionist expectations. With the leadership of an emerging Palestinian nationalism in the hands of the radical al-Husseinis, ideas such as the cooperation of the Jewish and Arab working classes in revolt against their capitalist overlords were buried by the more powerful attractions of nationalism and religion. Approaches such as that of Brit Shalom (Covenant of Peace) in the 1920s, which sought the permission and agreement of Arab nationalism to develop a bi-national solution, foundered because their Arab partners were few and far between. Martin Buber and Judah Magnes, passionate believers in bi-nationalism as a higher ideal, argued that either Jewish sovereignty or Arab sovereignty in Palestine was 'a questionable good'.[93] As late as 1945 the Zionist Left was putting forward the case for 'communal federalism' – a federation of the two national communities. The failure of such well-intentioned plans eventually left the liberal managerial approach of Weizmann and Ben-Gurion to gradually press ahead with Zionist aims while minimizing the clash with Arab nationalism. The other approach was that of Jabotinsky's fatalistic separatism and Begin's military Zionism, which overturned any notion of self-restraint.

What did the early Zionists think about the Arabs? The picture after 1882 is a mixed one. Many, like Herzl, were seemingly quite oblivious of the Arab presence. Others, including Ahad Ha'am, warned about the problems that lay ahead. Yet it is wrong to equate indifference and ignorance with racism. Herzl was the classic Central European liberal who vehemently condemned the slave trade and treatment of blacks. 'I am not ashamed to say that once I have witnessed the redemption of the Jews, my people, I wish also to assist in the redemption of the

Africans.'[94] In his utopian novel *Altneuland*, published in 1902, a 'New Society' of Arabs and Jews was being constructed. Yet it was more than an orientalist depiction of thankful Arabs and hard-working Jews, for it was 'a social vision based on universalism'.[95] Moreover Herzl bases his story on an election between the forces of reaction led by Rabbi Dr Geyer, who wishes to deprive the Arabs of their vote, and the enlightened liberal Zionists who eventually triumph at the polls. Herzl hardly took note of the rise of Arab nationalism, even in its embryonic stages, but the same cannot be said of Ahad Ha'am, who visited Palestine in 1891. In an article entitled 'Truth from the Land of Israel', he castigated the early settlers for their attitude towards the local Arabs and branded them with 'the arrogance of the slave-turned-master', writing: 'There is no one who stands up against this wrongful and dangerous behaviour. Our brothers may be right in saying that the Arabs respect only those who are tough with them – but if they have reason to think that they are being oppressed or persecuted, even if they say nothing and suppress their feelings until the end of time, they will harbour thoughts of revenge in their hearts.'[96]

Few followed Ahad Ha'am's path and most were seduced instead by Herzl's political Zionism. The prospect of reclaiming a resurgent Israel from the rubble of Jerusalem and freeing the Jews from the chains of history captured the imagination. It was perhaps the first step on a road which gradually replaced liberal internationalist Zionism with a security-conscious nationalism in which the idealism characterizing the notion that Israel should be 'a light unto the nations' was submerged by the rhetoric of patriotism and survivalism.

Weizmann believed that the immigrating Jews and the indigenous Arabs could work together for the good of the country. He seemed to believe the anti-Zionist Arabs were few and lived in the main towns in Palestine. In a private report to the Zionist Executive in November 1919, he wrote:

> The Arab is genuinely frightened of our immigration, not because he is anti-Jewish, because he was told that we are coming to take away his land. The Mufti of Jerusalem who is perhaps one of the most enlightened Arab gentlemen, who is honest and far from being fanatical, told me repeatedly that there was no room in Palestine for many more people to live. It was quite a revelation to him when I compared the density of population in Palestine with that of Lebanon. He was amazed to hear that with proper conditions of sanitation, irrigation and communication, the land could yield five, six or tenfold of what it is yielding now.[97]

Weizmann and many other Zionists had simply not taken sufficient note of the advance of Arab nationalism. Marxist Zionists, inspired by the birth of the Soviet Union, believed that solidarity between workers and economic amelioration would overcome all obstacles. The radicalism of the new Mufti of Jerusalem, Haj Amin al-Husseini, and the commitment of the younger generation of Palestinian notables to Arab nationalism were manifested in unrelenting opposition to Zionism. More accommodating elements such as the Nashashibis were ultimately silenced. Such rejectionism – ultimately of partition and a two-state solution – induced a strengthening of rejectionism on the Zionist side. Jabotinsky was perhaps the first to perceive the drawing of lines in the sand. In 1923 he argued that history recorded that it was immaterial whether settlers acted decently or not – he compared Cortés and Pizarro to the Pilgrim Fathers – in either case a native population would react. There was therefore a need for a defensive 'Iron Wall' of Jewish soldiers to protect settlers and settlements against Arab nationalist attacks. The situation negated the possibility of an immediate voluntary agreement, but it did not preclude one in the future:

> As long as the Arabs feel that there is the least hope of getting rid of us, they will refuse to give up this wish in return for either kind words or for bread and butter because they are not a rabble, but a living people. And when a living people yields in matters of such a vital character, it is only when there is no longer any hope of getting rid of us – because they can make no breach in the Iron Wall. Not until then will they drop their extremist leaders whose watchword is 'Never!' The leadership will pass to moderate groups who will approach us with a proposal that we should agree to mutual concessions. Then we may expect them to discuss honestly practical questions such as a guarantee against Arab displacement or equal rights for Arab citizens or Arab national integrity.[98]

Jabotinsky later argued that the Arabs had several states and it was not such a hardship for an Arab minority in an economically prosperous Jewish state. Indeed Palestine in the inter-war years had become a land of immigration rather than a land of emigration. Industrialization had attracted Arabs from both the interior and outside Palestine. The Arab population in Palestine grew twice as swiftly as those in Syria and Lebanon. Tens of thousands of Arabs entered Palestine from surrounding countries, increasing the population by 8%. The rate of growth of the Arab population of predominantly Jewish towns such as Haifa far exceeded the expectations of natural increase. Mindful of the growing deterioration of the situation in Eastern Europe in the late 1930s, Jabotinsky characterized the situation as that of Arab claims against Jewish needs. 'The claims of appetite,' he told the Peel Commission in 1937, 'versus the claims of starvation.'

Today Zionism is perceived in satanic terms on the Left and in a growing number of liberal forums as yet another example of European colonialism. This obscures the complex nature of Zionism and effectively severs the movement from the reasons for its genesis in Europe. The brand of Zionism that is considered today is one moored in Palestine and nowhere else. One-dimensional models do not work. Zionism is best perceived as 'historically and conceptually situated between colonial, anti-colonial and post-colonial discourse and practise'.[99] There are characteristics of the Zionist experiment which would attract different definitions but not define the whole. For example, simplistic approaches often ignore the role of British rule between 1918 and 1948 and the Zionist struggle against it.

The displacement of normative Religious Zionism by redemptionist groups such as *Gush Emunim* (Bloc of the Faithful) – guided by the teachings of Zvi Yehuda Kook – and by the religious settlers in general has led to a new Zionism since 1967 that is constrained neither by liberalism nor by universalism. If before 1967, Zionism was characterized by colonization, since 1967 its approach in the West Bank and Gaza has been defined by colonialism.

The conflict was previously interpreted as the struggles between the peace camps in both Israel and the Palestinian territories against their rejectionists. The European Left today prefers an easier, polarized image of Israel versus Palestine in which the Israeli peace camp and the Jewish national Left are relegated to the company of the walking dead. But the usefulness of Israeli dissent cannot be totally dismissed if it can aid the cause of Palestinian nationalism. This can only be rationalized if the dissenters can be de-Zionized and integrated into the broad international protest against Israeli government policies.

An extension of this mode of thought is to offer qualified support for a two-state solution, provided changes to the status quo are implemented which challenge 'the legitimacy of the state in its current form'.[100] This is more often an argument not for a return to 1967 and the evacuation of West Bank settlements, but a return to 1948 and the reversal of the Zionist experiment. Rather than a viable two-state solution of two sovereign peoples, it is a metaphor for a greater Palestine with a Jewish minority.

In a similar fashion those on the Left who hanker after the good old days of the Soviet Union proclaim their support for a two-state solution since the USSR supported the establishment of Israel. Yet this is qualified by a demand for the right of return of the Palestinians. If interpreted in absolute terms, this would mean the conversion of a Jewish majority in the state of Israel into a Jewish minority. The 'Israel' which would emerge would be one where the Jews no longer exercised their right to national self-determination. The multicultural comment that 'Israel should be a state of all its citizens' can also be viewed as a step on the path to a one-state solution with a Palestinian majority.

The stability of the Israeli state and the space provided by the hitherto optimism of the peace process have offered the possibility for alternative discourses in opposition to the normative Zionist one. New narratives which had formerly been omitted began to be related – the ultra-orthodox, women, Sephardi (Mizrachim) Jews and the Palestinians. As Michael Walzer has written about the traditional characterization of Zionist and Israeli history:

Every national liberation movement has to rewrite the history of
the nation it aims to liberate. A new history is always neces-
sary – so as to make liberation a more plausible project than it
is likely to appear, given the traditional history . . . the libera-
tionist historians have to 'untell' these stories and provide
different ones, commonly ones that celebrate heroism – even-
in-defeat and stubborn resistance thereafter and that are pointed
towards a national revival. We can see this in many cases, and
Zionism, despite all the peculiarities of Jewish life, is one of
them.[101]

It can be argued that the decision of the Likud government
to open the archives in the early 1980s was a subconscious
move to reclaim the story of the nationalist Right, which had
similarly been submerged by the Labour Zionist discourse.

The emergence of post-Zionism in Israel during the 1990s
was catalysed by the emergence of the 'new historians' and the
'critical sociologists' – popular labels but actually covering a
wide array of views and opinions. Although many post-Zionists
believed that Zionism was relevant in nineteenth-century
Eastern Europe, they argued that it had become obsolete in
twenty-first-century Israel. While some certainly embraced a
one-state solution to the question of Israel and Palestine or proposed that a de-Zionized Israel should be the state of all its
citizens, other post-Zionists supported the integrity of the state.
Even so, the current Intifada – and particularly the trauma of
suicide bombings – has placed any debate about post-Zionism
in cold storage.[102]

The rise of Islamism in Palestine under Hamas and Islamic
Jihad has undermined the influence of the peace camp in Israel
itself. Zionism is often characterized through anti-Semitic
stereotypes and portrayed as seeking to dominate the Arab

world through territorial expansion. The growing alliance between the European far Left and the Islamists is expressed ideologically in non-recognition of the Jews as a people. Both oppose any form of Jewish self-assertion and do not recognize any form of Jewish nationalism, including Zionism. Such a pattern was established during the Iranian revolution in 1979, when Islamists and Marxists collaborated in overthrowing the Shah. Khomeini then turned on his erstwhile allies and liquidated the Iranian Left.

Those who do not disavow the term 'Zionist' differentiate between a revolutionary phase which ended in 1948 and a post-revolutionary Zionism whose task now is to correct the distortions that have occurred along the way, as well as finding a solution to the conflict with the Palestinians.[103] This division also differentiates between those who accept the 1967 Green Line – or a modified version of it – as the border between Israel and Palestine and those who support settlement in the West Bank and Gaza. While the post-Zionists of every shade have moved the Israel–Palestine conflict to the centre of all debates about Zionism, today's Zionists continue to emphasize the achievement of building a new state and society in spite of all its observable imperfections and flaws. The archival revelations of the complexities of the 1948 war may have changed the narrative, but many have argued – among them the historian Benny Morris, who first used the declassified material – that this does not mean a break with Zionism per se, but only with the received wisdom propagated by Labour Zionism after 1948.

The Zionist saga as understood by many Jews in Israel did not end with the establishment of the state in 1948 or with the victory of the Six Day War in 1967. Zionism will have completed its task only when it repairs the past and refurbishes the present, when the Augean stables are cleaned and when a just society arises in Israel. In Europe, far away from the struggle of these national movements, 'anti-Zionist' has come to mean 'pro-Palestinian'. Yet many Zionists are 'pro-Palestinian' in seeking a genuine solution to the suffering of the Palestinians and a sovereign state of Palestine in the West Bank and Gaza. Ironically, the vested interests of the Palestinians in securing a viable state alongside Israel will be realized only if the liberal pragmatic vision of Zionism is allowed to complete its odyssey. Zionism was partly responsible for the birth of Palestinian nationalism. Given the opportunity, it will also be responsible for the birth of the Palestinian state.

Notes

1 Alexei Sayle, *Independent*, 3 October 2000.

2 Benny Morris, *The Birth of the Palestinian Refugee Problem 1947–1949*, Cambridge, 1987, p. 286.

3 Benny Morris, *The Birth of the Palestinian Refugee Problem Revisited*, Cambridge, 2004, p. 42.

4 Ibid., p. 60.

5 Colin Shindler, *The Triumph of Military Zionism: Nationalism and the Origins of the Israeli Right*, London, 2006, p. 11.

6 *New Statesman*, 19 March 2004.

7 *Guardian*, 7 February 2006.

8 *Jewish Chronicle*, 16 June 2006.

9 *Teheran Times*, 2 December 2004.

10 *Al Jazeera*, 23 February 2006.

11 Seumas Milne, *Guardian*, 9 May 2002.

12 Ian Baruma, *Guardian*, 17 October 2001.

13 Hassan Nasrallah quoted in Amal Saad-Ghorayeb, *Hizbullah: Politics and Religion*, London, 2002, p. 170.

14 *The Zionist*, 25 June 1926.

15 Shabtai Teveth, *Ben-Gurion: The Burning Ground 1886–1948*, Boston, 1987, pp. 233–5.

16 Eliahu Benyamini, *States for the Jews: Uganda, Birobidzhan and 34 Other Plans*, Tel Aviv, 1990.

17 Evyatar Friesel, 'New Zionism: Historical Roots and Present Meaning', *Studies in Zionism* 8 (2), 1987, pp. 187–9.

18 Nachum Goldman, *Memories*, London, 1970, p. 313.

19 David Ben-Gurion, 'Where There is No Vision, the People Perish', *Unease in Zion*, ed. Ehud Ben Ezer, Jerusalem, 1974, p. 71.

20 Babylonian Talmud, Order Nashim, Tractate Ketuvot 110b.

21 *The UJIA Study of Jewish Identity in the United Kingdom: A Survey of Jewish Parents*, London, 2004.

22 Chaim Weizmann's address at the 22nd Zionist Congress, Basel, 9 December 1946, published by the Jewish Agency, 1947.

23 Primo Levi, *Shema: Collected Poems of Primo Levi*, translated from the Italian by Ruth Feldman and Brian Swann, London, 1976.

24 *Guardian*, 26 April 1945.

25 A. Joseph Heckelman, *American Volunteers and Israel's War of Independence*, New York, 1974, p. 57.

26 Ezra Mendelsohn, *On Modern Jewish Politics*, Oxford, 1993, p. 3.

27 Babylonian Talmud, Order Nashim, Tractate *Kiddishin* 49b.

28 Robert Chazan, *European Jewry and the First Crusade*, Berkeley, 1987, p. 57.

29 Isaac M. Jost, *Geschichte der Israeliten*, IV, Vorwort, p. iii, Berlin, 1820–28, in Heinrich Graetz, *The Structure of Jewish History and other Essays*, ed. Ismar Schorsch, New York, 1975, p. 4.

30 Simon Dubnov, *History of the Jews*, vol. 1, New York, 1967, p. 380.

31 Isaiah 2:5.

32 Chaim Hisin, 'Mi yoman ehad ha Biluim' (From the 'Diary of One of the Bilu Members', Tel Aviv, 1925), quoted in *Encyclopaedia Judaica*, vol. 4, Jerusalem, 1972, p. 998.

33 Leon Trotsky, *The Tsarist Hosts at Work*, in Joseph Nedava, *Trotsky and the Jews*, Philadelphia, 1972, p. 55.

34 Leon Pinsker, *Auto-Emancipation: An Appeal to his People by a Russian Jew*, in Arthur Hertzberg, *The Zionist Idea: A Historical Analysis and Reader*, Philadelphia, 1997, p. 184.

35 *Rassvet*, nos. 31, 32 and 35 (1881), quoted in Louis Greenberg, *The Jews in Russia: The Struggle for Emancipation*, vol. II 1881–1917, New York, 1976, p. 56.

36 Correspondence from the town of Berezovka, Greenberg, p. 56.

37 Lucy Dawidowicz (ed.), *The Golden Treasury*, New York, 1967, p. 406.

38 Simon Dubnov, *History of the Jews*, vol. 5, New York, 1973, p. 590.

39 Moses Leib Lilienblum, *The Future of Our People* (1883), in Arthur Hertzberg, *The Zionist Idea: A Historical Analysis and Reader*, Philadelphia, 1997, p. 173.

40 Peretz Smolenskin, *Let Us Search our Ways* (1881), in Hertzberg, ibid., p. 150.

41 Chaim Weizmann, *Trial and Error*, London, 1949, p. 23.

42 Ahad Ha'am, 'Summa Summarum', translated from the Hebrew by Leon Simon, *Jewish Review*, May 1912.

43 Isaiah Berlin, *The Life and Opinions of Moses Hess,* in *Against the Current: Essays in the History of Ideas,* ed. Henry Hardy, London, 1979, p. 213.

44 Robert Fine, *Karl Marx and the Radical Critique of Anti-Semitism*, *Engage Journal*, no. 2, May 2006.

45 Isaiah Berlin, *The Life and Opinions of Moses Hess,* in *Against the Current: Essays in the History of Ideas,* ed. Henry Hardy, London, 1979, pp. 220–21.

46 Moses Hess, *Rome and Jerusalem*, ninth letter, New York, 1958, pp. 61–5.

47 Nachman Syrkin, 'An Appeal to Jewish Youth', *Jewish Frontier*, June 1935.

48 Vladimir Jabotinsky, *Jewish Chronicle*, 2 August 1929.

49 Vladimir Jabotinsky, 'Introduction to Chaim Nachman Bialik's *Poems from the Hebrew*', ed. L.V. Snowman, London, 1924.

50 Vladimir Jabotinsky, 'Shiva', *Yevreiskaya Zhizn*, no. 6, June 1904; *Hadar* (5–8), November 1940.

51 Ibid.

52 Vladimir Jabotinsky, 'Afn Pripitshek', *Haynt*, 16 October 1931; *Jewish Herald*, 12 September 1947.

53 Noah Lucas, *Israeli Nationalism and Socialism before and after 1948*, in *Israel: The First Decade of Independence*, ed. S. Ilan Troen and Noah Lucas, New York, 1995, p. 298.

54 Babylonian Talmud, Order Nashim, Tractate Ketuvot 111a.

55 Ahad Ha'am, 'The Jewish State and the Jewish Problem' (1897), in Arthur Hertzberg, *The Zionist Idea: A Historical Analysis and Reader*, Philadelphia, 1997, p. 266.

56 Ahad Ha'am, 'The Negation of the Diaspora' (1909), in Hertzberg, p. 270.

57 Nachum Sokolov, *History of Zionism*, London, 1919, pp. 162–3.

58 Samuel David Luzzatto, Letter to Albert Cohen (1854), in Richard J. H. Gottheil, *Zionism*, Philadelphia, 1914, p. 52.

59 Zvi Hirsch Kalischer, *Drishat Zion* (1863) in Arthur Hertzberg, *The Zionist Idea: A Historical Analysis and Reader*, Philadelphia, 1997, p. 114.

60 Chaim Weizmann, *Trial and Error*, London, 1949, p. 45.

61 *Yearbook of the Central Conference of American Rabbis 1897–1898*, p. 61.

62 David Vital, *A People Apart: The Jews in Europe 1789–1939*, Oxford, 1999, pp. 814–15.

63 Ludwig Geiger, *Die Stimme der Wahrheit*, Berlin, 1905, p. 165, in Richard J. H. Gottheil, *Zionism*, Philadelphia, 1914, p. 102.

64 Paul Mendes-Flohr and Jehuda Reinarz (eds.), *The Jew in the Modern World*, Oxford, 1995, p. 546.

65 Arthur Hertzberg, *The Fate of Zionism: A Secular Future for Israel and Palestine*, New York, 2003, p. 108.

66 Yosef Gorny, *The State of Israel in Jewish Public Thought: The Quest for Collective Identity*, London, 1994, p. 123.

67 Raphael Mahler, *A History of Modern Jewry 1780–1815*, London, 1971, p. 32.

68 Ibid., p. 44.

69 Rosa Luxemburg, 'Dyskusja', *Mlot*, no.14, 5 November 1910, in Robert S. Wistrich, *Revolutionary Jews: From Marx to Trotsky*, London, 1976, pp. 83–4.

70 J. L. Talmon, *Israel Among the Nations*, London, 1970, p. 96.

71 Max Nordau, Speech to the First Zionist Congress (1897), in Arthur Hertzberg, *The Zionist Idea: A Historical Analysis and Reader*, Philadelphia, 1997, p. 239.

72 Sa'adia Goldberg, in Benjamin West, *Struggles of a Generation: The Jews under Soviet Rule*, Tel Aviv, 1959, p. 155.

73 Robert Service, *Lenin: A Biography*, London, 2003, pp. 16–18.

74 Joseph Nedava, *Trotsky and the Jews*, Philadelphia, 1971, pp. 206–7.

75 Bertrand Russell, *Zionism and the Peace Settlement in Palestine: A Jewish Commonwealth in Our Time*, Washington, 1943, p. 18.

76 Michael Foot, *Aneurin Bevan 1945–1960*, London, 1975, p. 653.

77 Ibid., p. 416.

78 Noah Lucas, *Israeli Nationalism and Socialism before and after 1948*, in *Israel: The First Decade of Independence*, ed. S. Ilan Troen and Noah Lucas, New York, 1995, pp. 297–303.

79 Richard Crossman in a lecture given in Rechovot in April 1959, in *A Nation Reborn: The Israel of Weizmann, Bevin and Ben-Gurion*, London, 1960, p. 69.

80 Jonathan Freedland, *Guardian*, 18 October 2000.

81 Letter of Alastair Hetherington to Solly Sachs, 22 April 1971, in Geoffrey Taylor, *Changing Faces: A History of The Guardian 1956–1988*, London, 1993, p. 169. E. S. 'Solly' Sachs was a Communist and trade union leader from South Africa who was active during the 1960s and 1970s in attacking Zionist ideology.

82 *Guardian*, 14 May 1996.

83 *Al Ahram*, 4–10 April 2002.

84 Anthony Julius, 'Anti-Zionisms', a lecture delivered to the ICA, London, 24 June 2004.

85 David Lloyd-George, *Zionism and Antisemitism: The Absurd Folly of Jew-Baiting*, New York, 1923.

86 Bill Clinton, *My Life*, New York, 2004, p. 294.

87 Colin Shindler, 'Likud and the Christian Dispensationalists: A Symbiotic Relationship', *Israel Studies*, vol. 5 no. 1, Spring 2000, pp. 153–82.

88 Ibid., p. 173.

89 *Jerusalem Post*, 30 December 1996.

90 David Ben-Gurion, *Zichronot*, Tel Aviv, 1971, pp. 254–5.

91 Michael Lind, *New York Review of Books*, 2 February 1995.

92 Jacob Heilbrunn, *New York Review of Books*, 20 April 1995.

93 Martin Buber and Judah L. Magnes, *Arab-Jewish Unity*, London, 1947.

94 Golda Meir, *My Life*, New York, 1975, p. 309.

95 Shlomo Avineri, 'Zionism according to Theodor Herzl', *Ha'aretz*, 22 December 2002.

96 Yizhar Be'er, 'Prophets of Doom', *Ha'aretz*, 23 December 2002.

97 Chaim Weizmann, 'Our Relations with the Authorities', report to the Zionist Executive 7 November 1919, Herbert Samuel Archives, Oxford.

98 Vladimir Jabotinsky, 'The Iron Wall', *Rassvet*, 4 November 1923; *Jewish Herald*, 26 November 1937.

99 Derek J. Penslar, 'Zionism, Colonialism and Post-Colonialism', in *Israeli Historical Revisionism: From Left to Right*, ed. Anita Shapira and Derek J. Penslar, London, 2003, p. 85.

100 Seumas Milne, 'The Slur of Antisemitism is Used to Defend Repression', *Guardian*, 9 May 2002.

101 Michael Walzer, 'History and National Liberation', in Derek J. Penslar 'Zionism, Colonialism and Post-colonialism', in *Israeli Historical Revisionism: From Left to Right*, ed. Anita Shapira and Derek J. Penslar, London, 2003, p. 1.

102 Dalia Shehori, 'Post-Zionism is Dead or in a Deep Freeze', *Ha'aretz*, 20 April 2004.

103 Mordechai Bar-On, in Laurence J. Silberstein, *The Post-Zionism Debates: Knowledge and Power in Israeli Culture*, London, 1999, p. 53.

Glossary

Ahavat Tsion: The yearning for Zion

Aliyah: Emigration to Israel

Al-Nakhba: The Palestinian defeat, displacement and exodus in the war of 1948

Betar: Nationalist Zionist youth movement founded by Jabotinsky

Bund: Jewish socialist party opposed to Zionism

Dhimmi: protected but secondary status for Jews in Islamic society

Gush Emunim: Movement of religious West Bank settlers

Halutziut: The ethic of pioneering

Haskalah: The Jewish Enlightenment

Havlagah: Self-restraint in not responding to attacks on Jewish settlements

Husseinis: Family of Palestinian Arab notables which produced many nationalist leaders

Ilui: Child prodigy

Kabbalah: Jewish mysticism

Lubavich: A Hasidic dynasty, originally opposed to Zionism

Maskil (maskilim): Jewish enlightenment scholar

Muskeljudentum: Muscular Judaism

Narodnaya Volia: Russian revolutionary organization

Nashashibis: Family of Palestinian Arab notables opposed to the Husseinis

Risorgimento: Italian national movement

Ruzhiner: A Hasidic dynasty founded by Israel Friedmann

Umma: International community of Muslims

Wissenschaft des Judentums: Jewish scientific enquiry into traditional sources

Yishuv: The Jewish settlement in Palestine between 1882 and 1948

Yeshiva (yeshivot): religious seminaries

Yevsektsia: Jewish sections of the Bolshevik party

Who's Who in Zionism

Abba Achimeir (1898–1962) intellectual mentor of the Zionist maximalists

Yehuda Chai Alkalai (1798–1878) early progenitor of religious Zionism

Menachem Begin (1913–92) Prime Minister of Israel 1977–83

Yossi Beilin (1948–) architect of the Oslo Accords 1993; leader of the Meretz Party

Aneurin Bevan (1897–1960) creator of the British National Health Service

Chaim Nachman Bialik (1873–1934) Hebrew national poet

Nathan Birnbaum (1864–1937) originator of the term 'Zionism'

Dov Ber Borochov (1881–1917) founder and theorist of Marxism-Zionism

Isaac Adolphe Crémieux (1796–1880) president, Alliance Israélite Universelle

Richard Crossman (1907–74) British Minister 1964–70; editor *New Statesman*

Benjamin Disraeli (1804–81) British Prime Minister 1868, 1874–80

David Ben-Gurion (1886–1973) founding father of Israel; first Prime Minister 1949

Ahad Ha'am (Asher Hirsch Ginsburg) (1856–1927) Zionist intellectual and writer

A. D. Gordon (1856–1922) Zionist pioneer; Tolstoyan mentor of Labour Zionism

Judah Leib Gordon (1831–92) Hebrew poet and writer

Heinrich Graetz (1817–91) historian of the Jews and Bible scholar

Uri Zvi Greenberg (1894–1981) Zionist maximalist; Hebrew poet

Theodor Herzl (1860–1904) father of the modern Zionist movement

Moses Hess (1812–75) socialist theoretician; early progenitor of Socialist Zionism

Vladimir Jabotinsky (1880–1940) liberal nationalist; Revisionist Zionist, head of Betar

Isaac Jost (1793–1860) Jewish historian, writer and educator

Zvi Hirsch Kalischer (1795–1874) early progenitor of religious Zionism

Shimon Bar Kokhba (?-135) leader of the Jewish revolt against the Romans 132–5

Nachman Krochmal (1785–1840) Jewish historian, philosopher and writer

Ferdinand Lassalle (1825–64) founding father of German Socialism

Moses Leib Lilienblum (1843–1910) Hebrew writer, Zionist publicist and literary critic

David Lloyd-George (1863–1945)British Prime Minister 1916–22; Christian Zionist

Karl Lüeger (1844–1910) Viennese politician; leader Christian Social Party

Samuel David Luzzatto (1800–65) Italian Bible commentator and philosopher

Moses Mendelssohn (1729–86) German Enlightenment and Jewish philosopher

Moses Montefiore (1784–1885) leader of British Jewry; builder of Jerusalem

Bibi Netanyahu (1949–) Prime Minister of Israel 1996–9

Max Nordau (1849–1923) founder of the modern Zionist movement; writer and philosopher

Leon Pinsker (1821–91) Zionist leader, writer and publicist

Yitzhak Rabin (1922–95) Prime Minister of Israel 1974–7, 1992–5

Solomon Rapoport (1790–1867) *Haskalah* scholar, rabbi and writer

Walter Rathenau (1867–1922) German Foreign Minister, industrialist and writer

Yitzhak Reines (1839–1915) founder of Religious Zionism; first leader of Mizrachi

Ariel Sharon (1925–) Prime Minister of Israel 2001–6

Peretz Smolenskin (1842–85) *Haskalah* publicist; advocate of cultural nationalism

Hatam Sofer (Moses Schreiber) (1762–1839) leader of ultra-orthodoxy and scholar

Baruch Spinoza (1632–77) Dutch philosopher and exponent of biblical criticism

Nachman Syrkin (1868–1924) first leader of Socialist Zionism and ideologue

Yitzhak Tabenkin (1887–1971) founder of Labour Zionist and kibbutz movement

Leon Trotsky (1879–1940) Russian revolutionary and creator of the Red Army

Chaim Weizmann (1874–1952) founding father and first President of Israel 1949–52

Shneur Zalman of Lyady (1745–1813) founder of Lubavicher Hasidim

Timeline

66–70 First Jewish War against the Romans
70 Fall of Jerusalem and destruction of the Temple
638 Arab conquest of Jerusalem
642 Omar expels the Jews of Khaybar in Arabia
1099 Crusaders massacre the Jews of Jerusalem
1428 Pope forbids Italian ships to take Jews to Palestine
1492 Expulsion of Jews from Spain
1648 Chmielnicki massacres of Jews in the Ukraine
1656 Cromwell allows Jews to return to England
1789 French Revolution begins with the storming of the Bastille
1791 Pale of Settlement is established by Catherine the Great
1799 Napoleon invades Palestine from Egypt
1836 Zvi Hirsch Kalischer attempts to purchase territory in Palestine
1860 Theodor Herzl is born in Budapest
1863 *Rome and Jerusalem* by Moses Hess is published
1881 Pogroms in Russia follow the assassination of the Tsar
1882 *Auto-Emancipation* by Leon Pinsker is published
1882 First wave of emigration from Russia to Palestine begins
1894 Trial of Alfred Dreyfus takes place in France
1896 *The Jewish State* by Theodor Herzl is published
1897 First Zionist Congress takes place in Basel
1898 Nachman Syrkin advocates Socialist Zionism and attacks Herzl
1901 Weizmann's Democratic Faction advocates a non-religious Zionist education
1902 Religious Zionists establish Mizrachi

1903 Uganda plan as a temporary substitute for Palestine splits the Zionist movement

1904 Herzl dies

1906 Ben-Gurion and Ben-Zvi establish the Labour Zionist Poale Zion in Palestine

1909 First collective settlement is established in Palestine

1912 Agudat Yisrael, party of the ultra-orthodox opposed to Zionism, is established

1914 World War I begins

1915 Joseph Trumpledor forms the Zion Mule Corps, which sees action at Gallipoli

1917 Vladimir Jabotinsky establishes the Jewish Legion

1917 Arthur Balfour promises a national home for the Jewish people in Palestine

1917 Lenin and Trotsky stage Bolshevik *coup d'état* in Russia

1919 Labour Zionist party Achdut Ha'avodah founded by Ben-Gurion

1920 Histadrut, the General Federation of Labour in Israel, founded

1921 Transjordan, the eastern part of Mandatory Palestine, is promised to Abdullah

1925 Jabotinsky establishes the Union of Revisionist Zionists

1930 Mapai, the Labour Zionist party, is founded

1936 Arab Revolt breaks out in Palestine

1938 Neville Chamberlain promises 'peace in our time' after meeting Hitler

1939 World War II begins with the invasion of Poland

1942 Systematic mass extermination of Jews begins in occupied Europe

1944 Menachem Begin, commander of the Irgun Zvai Leumi, proclaims the Revolt

1945 Liberation of the Nazi concentration camps after six million Jews are exterminated

1947 Second partition of Palestine into a Jewish and an Arab state

1948 State of Israel is proclaimed amidst a bitter conflict with the Palestinian Arabs

1949 First elections take place in Israel

1956 Suez crisis involves collusion between Israel, France and Britain

1967 Israel defeats the armies of Egypt, Jordan and Syria in the Six Day War

1973 Egypt launches surprise crossing of the Suez Canal during the Yom Kippur War

1977 Election of Menachem Begin as Prime Minister of Israel

1979 Begin and President Anwar Sadat of Egypt sign the Camp David Accords

1981 Sadat is assassinated

1982 Invasion of Lebanon by Israeli troops under Ariel Sharon

1987 First Intifada breaks out

1992 Election of Yitzhak Rabin as Prime Minister of Israel

1993 Rabin and Yasser Arafat, leader of the Palestine Liberation Organisation, sign the Oslo Accords

1995 Yitzhak Rabin is assassinated

1996 Election of Bibi Netanyahu as Prime Minister of Israel

1999 Election of Ehud Barak as Prime Minister of Israel

2000 Breakdown of Camp David negotiations; outbreak of al-Aqsa Intifada

2000 Clinton Parameters for the resolution of the Israel–Palestine conflict are formulated

2001 Election of Ariel Sharon as Prime Minister of Israel

2003 Sharon commences a disengagement plan for the evacuation of Israeli settlements

2004 Arafat dies

2005 Abu Mazen is elected President of the Palestinian Authority

2006 Hamas defeats Al Fatah in elections for the Legislative Council

2006 Election of Ehud Olmert as Prime Minister of Israel

2006 Month long conflict between Israel and Hezbollah in Lebanon

Further Reading

Shmuel Almogi, Jehuda Reinharz and Anita Shapira, *Zionism and Religion*, Hanover, 1998

Shlomo Avineri, *The Making of Modern Zionism*, London, 1981

Dov Ber Borochov, *Class Struggle and the Jewish Nation: Selected Essays in Marxist Zionism*, London, 1984

Mitchell Cohen, *Zion and State: Nation, Class and the Shaping of Modern Israel*, Oxford, 1987

Alain Dieckhoff, *The Invention of a Nation: Zionist Thought and the Making of Modern Israel*, London, 2003

Ahad Ha'am, *Nationalism and the Jewish Ethic: Basic Writings of Ahad Ha'am*, New York, 1962

Ben Halpern, *The Idea of a Jewish State*, Harvard, 1969

Arthur Hertzberg, *The Zionist Idea*, Philadelphia, 1997

Moses Hess, *Rome and Jerusalem*, New York, 1917

Rael Jean Isaac, *Israel Divided: Ideological Politics in the Jewish State*, Baltimore, 1976

Jacques Kornberg, *Theodor Herzl: From Assimilation to Zionism*, Bloomington, 1993

Walter Laqueur, *History of Zionism*, London, 2003

Benny Morris, *The Birth of the Palestinian Refugee Problem Revisited*, Cambridge, 2004

Leon Pinsker, *Road to Freedom: Writings and Addresses*, Westport, 1975

Jehuda Reinharz, *Chaim Weizmann: The Making of a Zionist Leader*, Oxford, 1985

Jehuda Reinharz, *Chaim Weizmann: The Making of a Statesman*, Oxford, 1993

Howard M. Sachar, *History of Israel: From the Rise of Zionism to Our Time*, New York, 1996

Gabriel Sheffer, *Moshe Sharett: Biography of a Political Moderate*, Oxford, 1996

Colin Shindler, *The Triumph of Military Zionism: Nationalism and the Origins of the Israeli Right*, London, 2006

Sasson Sofer, *Begin: Anatomy of a Leadership*, Oxford, 1988

Chaim Weizmann, *Trial and Error*, London, 1949

Steven J. Zipperstein, *Elusive Prophet: Ahad Ha'am and the Origins of Zionism*, London, 1993

Index